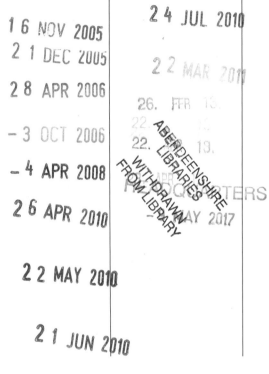
TREMAYNE, David

Rubens Barrichello

D0257902

Rubens
BARRICHELLO

Rubens
BARRICHELLO

**In the spirit of Senna and the
shadow of Schumacher**

David Tremayne

Foreword by **Johnny Herbert**

First published in June 2005

A catalogue record for this book is
available from the British Library

ISBN 1 84425 200 0

Library of Congress control no. 2005921424

Published by Haynes Publishing, Sparkford,
Yeovil, Somerset, BA22 7JJ, UK
Tel: 01963 442030 Fax: 01963 440001
Int. tel: +44 1963 442030 Int. fax: +44 1963 440001
E-mail: sales@haynes.co.uk
Website: www.haynes.co.uk

Haynes North America, Inc.,
861 Lawrence Drive, Newbury Park,
California 91320, USA

All images supplied by sutton-images.com

Layout by G&M Designs Limited,
Raunds, Northamptonshire
Printed and bound in England by
J. H. Haynes & Co. Ltd, Sparkford

CONTENTS

FOREWORD

When I won the 1999 Grand Prix of Europe at the Nürburgring for Stewart Grand Prix, Rubens Barrichello, my teammate, was the first man to congratulate me. He was delighted that I had won. He had finished third, making it a great day for Jackie Stewart and his son Paul. But I knew that Rubens must have been extremely disappointed not to have been the man to deliver their first win, having come close several times earlier that season. Yet there was not the slightest hint of 'I wish it had been me', in his manner towards me. He was genuinely happy.

To me, that was typical of Rubens. I got on well at Lotus driving alongside Mika Häkkinen and Alex Zanardi, but I would say Rubens was the best teammate I ever had. He was totally honest and friendly, and you always knew where you were with him. We had similar driving styles and temperaments, and were able to work together. I had a lot of respect for him, and him for me.

Having been Michael Schumacher's teammate at Benetton in 1995, I also have a very keen grasp of what Rubens has faced in his time at Ferrari. He went there with absolute passion for the team and its heritage, whereas Michael didn't ever have that. Rubens was there because of that passion, and sometimes in his early days at Maranello his Latin temperament got the better of him. But one of the nicest things is how he has matured, not just since his early days at Jordan, but during his time at Ferrari. He is better at keeping some things to himself now, and at dealing with the fact that Michael Schumacher is … well, Michael Schumacher. As we both know, Michael has a unique style of working that does not always help his teammate, let's say. It seems to me that at times that Rubens has had a mid-season slump, only to pick up form once Michael has won the title; the man I knew as my partner at Stewart was always very consistent, in my opinion. He never had an off day. Now Rubens just gets on with the job, and he does it very well. He is one of the toughest teammates Michael has ever had. He's risen to the challenge that Michael poses, and has improved himself.

He's done a cracking job.

I first met David Tremayne long before my own F1 career began. He is a loyal ally who has a great passion for the sport and understands drivers and their motivations and aspirations. In this book he has captured the essence of the Rubens Barrichello I know perfectly.

Johnny Herbert
Fontveille
April 2005

INTRODUCTION

My nephew has an intriguing photograph in his study. In many ways it is unique, capturing a remarkable day in motorsport history when an underdog scored a brilliant triumph. In the centre stands Jackie Stewart, arms aloft holding yet another trophy. But it is not taken at the time of one of the Scot's one-time record 27 grands prix victories as a driver and triple world champion, for he was never an underdog at the wheel. To Stewart's right stands Johnny Herbert, who was the victor that day, 26 September 1999, driving a Ford-powered car that bore the Stewart name in the Grand Prix of Europe at the 'new' Nürburgring, a stone's throw from the grand 'old' Nürburgring on which, 31 years earlier, Stewart had scored the most remarkable of his victories in rain and fog. Herbert has inscribed a message of thanks for my nephew's work with him at Ford.

To Stewart's left stands Rubens Barrichello. Where Herbert (unusually, for him) has been effusive in his thanks, Barrichello's signed comment is somewhat simpler. 'To Andrew,' it says, 'Bastard, bastard, bastard!'

That should not be taken literally (as family I can provide proof, whatever others may insist). But it captures the little Brazilian's carefree and affectionate sense of humour.

The former journalist Stéphane Samson wrote a strong insight into his character for *F1 Racing* magazine in 2004 in which he recounted an occasion when he was with the Brazilian at Paris Charles de Gaulle Airport as a fellow passenger recognised him and politely asked if he would mind speaking on the 'phone to the man's seven-year-old son. It was his birthday, and he would just be getting ready for school in Montreal. Without hesitation Barrichello complied, and one can only wonder, once the father had finally persuaded his child that it really had been the Ferrari driver wishing him happy birthday on the 'phone, at the boost that must have given the boy.

Up and down the pit lane, you'll struggle to find anybody with a genuinely bad word to say about Barrichello, a multilingual, open-hearted little guy who looks like Kelsey Grammer from the US television series *Frasier*, is rarely seen without a smile half a metre wide and conducts his high profile life in a stylish, non-materialistic manner. Sure, there are those who believe in his talent (among them Stewart) and those who don't; those who reckon he is the toughest teammate Michael Schumacher has ever had and those who see him as little more than the German champion's willing stooge. But as far as his character is concerned, they all know that what you see is what you get, and what you do see is one of the sport's nice guys. There is no side to Barrichello. He is genuine and sincere in his beliefs, and in the few criticisms that circumstances sometimes provoke from him. And he is a sound role model: the product of a loving family who is himself a family man who dotes on his wife Sylvana and young son Eduardo. He has a very big heart, and he is not afraid to wear it on his sleeve.

In the commercialism of Formula One's grasping, dog-eat-dog milieu, all of these traits are to be prized.

ACKNOWLEDGEMENTS

No one source can provide all the information for a book on a driver who is heading into his 13th season in Formula One, so it is with gratitude that I acknowledge the great assistance, in the form of recollections, anecdotes, opinions and/or straight quotes, that I received from the following: Gary Anderson; Rubens Barrichello himself; Dick Bennetts; Ross Brawn; Martin Brundle; David Coulthard; Johnny Herbert; Warren Hughes; Eddie Jordan; Luca di Montezemolo; Andrew Philpott; Joe Saward; Sir Jackie Stewart; Paul Stewart; Roberto Trevisan; Richard West; and Daniela Zanardi.

I also thank *Autocourse* annual, the *crash.net* website, and *F1 Racing* magazine for permission to use quotes.

PROLOGUE:
FRIDAY, IMOLA 1994

It was, Richard West knew immediately, an accident rather than just a shunt.

It was 29 April 1994. That afternoon, shortly after lunch, West had made his way from the pits down to one of the grandstands at the Autodromo Enzo e Dino Ferrari in Imola. It was on the outside of the Variante Bassa, the silly little chicane at the end of the lap which West referred to as the Bus Stop. He had been in Formula One a long time, working for McLaren and now for Rothmans-sponsored Williams-Renault. In his role as director of sponsorship and marketing services for Sir Frank Williams's team it was his job to look after every aspect of the sponsorship deals. He had suggested the walk down to the grandstand to Bertie Gaertner (the senior director of Rothmans with whom he and Williams had signed the deal the previous autumn) and event manager Dawn Lemon, so they could watch the first qualifying session of the San Marino Grand Prix. It was Gaertner's first trip to a Formula One race, and one of Rothmans' drivers was the legendary Ayrton Senna who was fighting hard to open his points score and to beat the upstart Michael Schumacher who, against predicted form, had won the two opening events in his Benetton Ford. West would point out salient factors to Gaertner and Lemon, offering an exclusive and knowledgeable insider's view that would enhance their understanding and enjoyment. It was a harder job than it might have seemed to the other spectators who sat around them, but for all that it was not one in which West expected their lives to be threatened. And certainly not by one of the most affable drivers in the paddock.

The drama came upon the three of them the way many dramas occur in motor racing, suddenly and with virtually no warning. Even back then the cars travelled fantastically fast, so much so that no human eye could detect untoward movement and react to it fast enough to avoid disaster.

Spectators in West's grandstand discovered this the frightening way when suddenly from the track a screaming, whirling blur of red and blue and grey and black came barrelling not through the Variante Bassa, but instead straight towards them. There was no time to react. By the time anyone in the grandstand figured out that something had gone terribly wrong, the demon was already panting its fiery breath upon them.

In the cockpit of Jordan number 14, Rubens Barrichello had no more time to think any thoughts than West had. From the moment the car snatched itself from his control, he was merely a passenger. His smooth-handling race car had suddenly become a terrifyingly high-speed missile.

It was a warm afternoon as the sun filtered lazily down on the Autodromo Enzo e Dino Ferrari. The first official qualifying session for the Grand Prix was only 16 minutes old as the Brazilian came down through Imola's two left-handed Rivazza curves and headed into the last section of the lap, the tricky little Variante Bassa. This was nothing more than a chicane (*variante* in Italian), a right-left flick taken at very high speed. Barrichello had gone through it many times in his career, and already knew it well from his first Grand Prix at the circuit the previous season, and from his days racing in the GM Lotus Euroseries in 1990. That morning he had lapped his Jordan in 1m 24.508s, a competitive time which stood him tenth fastest then, and would have been good enough to have left him 17th on the grid had it been an official session. It was comfortably faster than temporary teammate Andrea de Cesaris would go all weekend. But now he made a small but crucial error, running a fraction too wide past the kerb on the right-hand side as he went into the first part of the chicane.

In a split second the Jordan flicked on to oversteer and suddenly, instead of being nicely lined up for the left-hand part, it was heading to the right, straight for the grandstand in which West and his companions were sitting. The inside kerb launched it four feet into the air and it was so high that it cleared the concrete retaining wall that was faced by a protective red-and-white wall of old tyres, five deep. Still travelling at undiminished speed, it hit the 20-foot high heavy steel hawser safety fence that was designed to protect spectators in the grandstand. Both right-hand wheels struck the fence, the right front being torn off and actually landing behind the safety fence, in the spectator area. Mercifully, it didn't hit anyone. As the steel hawsers flexed upon impact, the latent energy within them threw the Jordan back on to the track, as if it was a toy thrown by the hand of a petulant giant. It nosedived back to the ground before barrel rolling once and losing its right rear wheel too. In the cockpit Barrichello sat slumped, his right arm flailing helplessly in the airstream until finally the shattered hulk came to a smoking rest.

The sheer violence of the accident was horrific, a terrible reminder of the savage force which had torn apart Martin Donnelly's Lotus at Jerez three years earlier, or Alex Zanardi's Lotus at Spa the previous year.

Observers feared for Barrichello's life.

'Rubens was obviously beginning to go very quickly, and just as he went into the right-hand section of the corner there was the squeal of a tyre,' West remembered. 'That was what alerted me. There's a photo somebody took where the right-hand front wheel of Rubens's car is just about to hit the safety fence, and in the background you can see the three of us diving down. I'd seen accidents before and been involved in them – I was there on the pit wall in Mexico in 1988 when Philippe Alliot tossed his Larrousse Lola into the wall and it made a noise like a bomb exploding. As soon as I saw something was wrong I dived down but had to grab Bertie and Dawn because they were just sitting bolt upright, unaware what was happening. Because I'm quite a big bloke I ended up covering them with my body. What I remember most was the sickening noise – that horrible crump. In that split-second I thought, "Shit, that must really have hurt." I knew straight away that it was a lot worse than a racing driver's shunt.'

Professor Sid Watkins, the FIA medical delegate who was always out on track in the medical car whenever the race cars were out, arrived on the scene within 15 seconds, having been parked close to the entry to Variante Bassa. Watkins, and nearby marshals, had actually started in motion before the shattered Jordan came fully to rest.

Within five minutes Barrichello had been stabilised and removed from the cockpit. He was then taken to the medical centre in the circuit's paddock, before being transferred to the Maggiore Hospital in Bologna for routine tests and observation.

'I heard David Brown, a Williams engineer, and Frank talking over the radio through my headset,' West continued, 'and I reported that Rubens was still in the car. There was a lot of blood coming from his nostrils. Sid was there, and they fitted Rubens with a neck brace and then he was taken to the medical centre. Bertie was so shaken, and Dawn was just so non-plussed by it all, that we went back to the motorhome so Bertie could have a cigarette and a brandy.'

When that news broke in the press room it was a massive relief, for Barrichello's accident bore all the terrible hallmarks of tragedy such was its violence. Soon the news filtered through that his injuries were confined to retrograde amnesia after he had been knocked unconscious by the initial impact, a cracked rib, and a broken nose, and some unpleasant but ultimately superficial (in the scheme of things) facial cuts where his head had hit the side of the cockpit when the car hit the safety fence. This was immediately seized upon as testament to the strength of the modern Formula One car, and indeed this was so. The Jordan had stood up brilliantly to an impact that would probably have been fatal in previous years.

'I think the problem was that normally Rubens would attack *after* that corner, as he went into a quick lap,' Jordan's chief engineer Gary Anderson (a strong supporter of Barrichello's) suggested. 'That lap he started pushing as he went *into* the Variante Bassa, but he hadn't gone really hard through it up to that point of the weekend so he didn't really know what to expect. He'd only just done his out lap. It looked as though he was a little wide turning into the right-hand section of the chicane, and there may still have been a little oil down there from a problem Mika Häkkinen had with his engine there in the morning session.'

The Finn's McLaren had caught fire there during morning free practice after one of the oil pipes on its Peugeot engine had detached itself, prompting spectating FIA president Max Mosley to declare: 'It's his afterburner!'

'Rubens's right-hand front wheel came back and brushed his helmet,' Anderson continued in his analysis of the accident, 'but the real damage was done when his head hit the side of the tub.'

Barrichello arrived back at the circuit under his own power the following day. Holding up his bandaged right arm, his upper lip unshaven because of the bruising round his nose, he showed off his injuries to his friends in the paddock before heading back to his home in Cambridge. There was no question of him racing that weekend. 'I don't know what happened,' he admitted. 'But I think I was quick! I feel okay – it's just a bit difficult to breathe because of my nose, and my hand hurts a bit, but otherwise I'm okay. I'm off to play with the nurses now!'

He was bruised and battered, but unbowed. Able, even, to laugh about the terrifying experience. It is still, thankfully, the biggest accident he has experienced to date.

'That weekend had a life of its own,' West suggested, echoing the sentiments of many who were there. 'It did what it did, and everyone was just a passenger.'

Rubens Barrichello's own ride on that terrible express was already over, but what would happen over the remainder of that fateful weekend in Imola would shape everything that he came to feel and believe in as his Formula One career blossomed.

Chapter 1

BEGINNINGS, AND A RIVALRY: RACING IN BRAZIL, 1981–9

On 14 May 1972, Frenchman Jean-Pierre Beltoise drove his BRM to a remarkable triumph in the Monaco Grand Prix on the rain-soaked streets of Monte Carlo. A fortnight later, on 4 June, Brazilian Emerson Fittipaldi took his Lotus to victory on the sterile waste of Nivelles in the Belgian Grand Prix.

In between, Arturo Merzario and Sandro Munari won for Ferrari in the Targa Florio sports car classic in Sicily, leading home a brace of Alfa Romeos driven by Helmut Marko and Nanni Galli, and Andrea de Adamich and Toine Hezemans.

Two days later, on 23 May, a Tuesday, far across the globe in Sao Paulo, Rubens Barrichello and his wife celebrated the birth of their son. Coincidentally, it was Rubens Snr's birthday.

If that son had grown up to be a Champ Car driver rather than a Formula One star, and had been named in American style, he would actually have been Rubens Barrichello Jnr Jnr, since his father was also named after his own paternal parent. Rubao, then a youthful 22 years old, never raced himself but would be as supportive of his son's competitive efforts as American legends Mario Andretti and Al Unser Snr were of their respective offspring, Michael and Al Jnr. And whenever the young Rubinho's career fell into a rut and he experienced emotional highs and desperate lows, the extraordinarily close relationship he enjoys with his father would never be more crucial nor more sustaining. Racing fathers can be an unusual and generally pushy breed, but Rubens Snr is obviously a man apart.

'My father has been very good to me, because he's not like the type of father who says you must do this or that, and that's it, you know?' Barrichello says, his face immediately breaking into its trademark wide smile. 'So my father didn't come to me, even when I was six and racing go-karts, he never would come and say, "Do this, this, or this." Because we learned together. He never did any racing himself. His sport was football, he was a goalkeeper. With me he was just a very big friend. We decided our future, and he just helped me. We are very similar. I don't know if it's just because I was born on the same day as him. We are very similar, and we do things together.'

You don't spend much time in Barrichello's company before the closeness of the family bond becomes evident. The boy is a man now, but he and his father still have an incredibly close bond and Rubinho credits his father with much of his education outside of school.

'I give a lot of credit to him, and he gives me a lot as well. Sometimes we have problems as normal, because we get confused: for instance, one year, were we talking as the manager to the driver, or the father to the son? We were confusing this. Sometimes the manager was talking to the son, sometimes the driver was talking to the father. That didn't make sense. Or sometimes I would go home upset with something, and I would change his afternoon because I was feeling bad and was not very good. So, we had this type of problem, but it was a very minor thing. We would sort it out, no problem.

'I have a very good relationship with him, and that made me feel so good that I could sit in the car and know that everything was working right, because he did most of the things for me. He is the person I would invite to sleep in my car, in my home, he is the person I would invite to go to the cinema. He is the person I would invite to go everywhere with me because he is good to me. He is really good. Even if I qualify last, he is always there to give me some words of encouragement.'

Yet it was not Rubens Snr who encouraged his son to go into motor racing. That fell to Mrs Barrichello's brother, Darcio dos Santos, Rubinho's uncle, who was himself a racing driver. Barrichello grew up in the Interlagos neighbourhood of Sao Paulo, where the city's motorsport fraternity is based, and was soon racing karts.

'It was Uncle Darcio who really got me started. Because he was a driver we would sometimes go to races together when I was a little kid, because of his enthusiasm for it. It was his father who gave me my first go-kart. The Barrichello family never raced.'

Rubens Snr began taking his son to tracks so that he could test the kart, but then a degree of friction arose. 'My father thought I wasn't ready to race. After one year of testing my uncle told me if I could break the barrier of one minute round one circuit, I was ready. The brothers of my father were the ones who took me that day. I was eight years old and I broke the barrier, and my father still said I wasn't ready, but Uncle Darcio put me into the race, paid for the fee, and I finished third. And they called my father and told him I was on the podium! Now that I have a son, I would be really pissed off if something happened to me like that!'

Despite that, the relationship between father and son remained strong and they went racing in earnest. Soon Rubinho was winning Cadet races, before graduating to the junior category. It was during his karting career that his rivalry with fellow Sao Paulista Christian Fittipaldi began.

In Brazilian motorsport lore, the Fittipaldis were gods. Emerson had graduated to Europe in 1969, intending initially to stay for three months until the money ran out. He dominated Formula Ford so easily in a Merlyn that mentor Jim Russell, the famed driving school owner, pushed him into a Lotus 59 in Formula Three that same year. When 20-year-old Fittipaldi immediately kept on winning, Lotus chief Colin Chapman, still mourning the great Jim Clark after the Scot's death in 1968, took serious interest. By 1970 Fittipaldi was racing for Lotus in Formula Two. By the British Grand Prix in July he had made his

Formula One debut, finishing eighth, and backed that with fourth next time out in Germany. After world champion-elect Jochen Rindt was killed in his Lotus at Monza that September, it was Fittipaldi who led the shattered Lotus team back into racing with victory in the US Grand Prix at Watkins Glen that October. It was only his fourth grand prix, and his success in keeping contender Jacky Ickx off the top step of the podium there cemented the title for Rindt, who thus became the sport's only posthumous champion. Even the gentlemanly Ickx was relieved.

Formula One was used to South Americans of Argentinian birth, after the stellar performances of the legendary Juan Manuel Fangio (and his doughty compatriot Froilan Gonzales) in the 1950s, but Fittipaldi was the man who blazed the trail for Brazil. After winning two world titles (the first – in 1972, the year of Barrichello's birth – making him, at 25, the youngest champion until one Michael Schumacher relieved him of that record much more controversially in 1994) he became a hero in the land of his birth. Not long afterwards, taller and older brother Wilson joined Emerson, first in Europe, and then in Formula One, as did their friend Jose-Carlos Pace. And subsequently hundreds of their young countrymen were inspired to try and emulate their performances.

In the intervening years Nelson Piquet Souto-Maior (who raced as Nelson Piquet) and Ayrton Senna da Silva (who raced as Ayrton Senna) also followed along the yellowbrick road, each winning three world championship titles.

And now here was Christian Fittipaldi, Wilson's son and Emerson's nephew, hell-bent on upholding family honour. This good-looking, dashing young man was a year older than Rubens and had been racing a year longer. Rubinho knew that if he beat this latest thoroughbred from the Fittipaldi stable, he would quickly build a reputation as another upcoming Brazilian heading for the big time. Often they clashed on the track, such was the intensity of their competitive ardour. But there was one time, in a kart race at Interlagos, when it was the fathers, Rubens Snr and

Wilson, who got into a frantic argument in the pits, screaming and shouting at one another. A few yards away their two sons were for once occupying themselves with a pastime more in keeping with their tender age, flying kites and completely oblivious to their parents' spat.

Christian Fittipaldi quit karting a year sooner than Barrichello, because of his seniority. They didn't meet up again until 1990, when they raced in South American F3 at Interlagos. Barrichello was victorious, literally pipping hotshoe Oswaldo Negri, who had raced with some distinction in Europe, as they crossed the finish line. The rivalry between Barrichello and Fittipaldi was tangible, but that day they embraced warmly, as Rubinho's win (in his third Formula Three outing) had secured the championship title for Fittipaldi. Witnessing their unusual affection, Fittipaldi's grandmother Dona Juzy was moved to comment: 'Isn't it good to see two boys hugging each other after so much quarrelling?'

Barrichello had begun racing at the age of nine in 1981 when he entered the Sao Paulo City Junior Karting Championship. He finished the season in the runner-up slot, and by 1983 had won the title and the Brazilian Junior Karting Championship. The Brazilian Olympic Committee voted him the Best Amateur Driver of the Year, and the Sao Paulo Municipal Secretary of Sports voted him Sao Paulo's Best Driver (though one wonders what Senna, newly crowned that season's British F3 champion, might have thought of that).

Barrichello won the Junior Karting Championship again in 1984, and graduated to the 'B' category the following year, when he won the Sao Paulo City Championship and finished fourth in the national series. He topped off another strong year by winning the Interlagos Tournament, a special event organised in celebration of 25 years of karting in Brazil.

In 1986, while fellow countryman Maurizio Sandro Sala was the hot prospect in British F3, Barrichello graduated to the 'A' category and promptly dominated it. He won both the Sao Paulo City and Brazilian National Championships, and repeated the feat in 1987 and 1988. In 1987 he also added the South American 125cc Championship to his growing list of successes, and finished ninth in the World Karting Championship. He was still only 15 years old.

When a driver finally ends up racing for Scuderia Ferrari stories always appear describing how they knew they wanted to drive the red cars even in their most formative years. Barrichello would become one of the rare stars who made it through to do just that, but years later he related a tale about testing one day at Interlagos which suggested his childhood dream involved a different marque. 'It's quite funny. I was about six and was driving my go-kart there and Renault rented the circuit and they were running, so all of a sudden I became a Renault fan! That was way back. But later, as a racing driver, you always think about the red cars. I think there is no way for you to avoid that.'

In 1989 he took the next step on the path to Maranello. The only way to go was single-seater racing cars, and with the support of Arisco, a national food company, he entered the Brazilian Formula Ford Championship with Team Arisco, and finished the season fourth overall. During the winter he tested a Formula Opel Lotus.

Along the way, Uncle Darcio had given Rubinho plenty of advice, but they had never met together on the track until that winter at Interlagos. Darcio was testing his Formula Three car, Barrichello a Formula Opel Lotus. Rubinho settled in after a handful of laps, and promptly went quicker than his uncle managed even though his car had greater grip and power.

It had long been obvious to seasoned observers that Rubens Barrichello was something special. Now they felt that the young rising star was ready for the next major challenge: to follow in the wheeltracks of the Fittipaldis, Pace, Piquet, and Senna, and head for the hallowed race tracks of Europe.

Chapter 2

ANOTHER BOY FROM BRAZIL: RACING IN EUROPE, 1990–2

Barrichello had some big very big footprints in which to follow as he moved to Europe in 1990, but he graduated seamlessly to the GM Formula Opel Lotus Euroseries. He had plentiful financial backing from Arisco, which was keen to grow with its promising star as they planned to work together all the way up to Formula One. It was the ideal situation for a young man in a hurry, who could thus put all monetary worries behind him and concentrate 100 per cent on doing everything the right way as he learned more about racing in an unfamiliar world.

Very soon Barrichello began to cut the same well-heeled path through Europe that his illustrious compatriots had blazed in their early days. Driving for the Italian Draco Racing team in the simple single-seater cars manufactured by Reynard, he quickly became a winner. Overall he took six victories, seven pole positions, and set seven fastest laps on his way to winning the title at his first attempt. On the way he beat another upcoming Brazilian of whom much was expected – Gil de Ferran – and Italian rising star Vincenzo Sospiri.

With all the financial matters sorted out, there was only one logical port of call for 1991. Barrichello beat a path to the door of West Surrey Racing, the Formula Three team that had taken his countrymen Ayrton Senna and Mauricio Gugelmin to the prestigious British Formula Three championship. West Surrey was run by New Zealander Dick Bennetts, an immensely likeable and talented fellow known within the sport as 'The Guru' because of his encyclopaedic knowledge of the technical side of

F3. Bennetts might not be anywhere near the front of the grid when it came to making decisions in a hurry, because of his penchant for examining things minutely from each and every angle, but there was nobody else in the game who knew as much as he did about getting the most from the driver/car package. Barrichello already knew Ayrton Senna, and the champion did not hesitate to recommend his friend to Bennetts.

Typically, Bennetts prevaricated for weeks whether to go for Reynard's new 913 chassis, or to stick with the trusty Ralt marque with which he had achieved so much. In the end, Barrichello was given a brand new Ralt RT35 with Mugen Honda power to drive. It was an evolution of the car in which Finnish rising star Mika Häkkinen had won the title the previous year with Bennetts.

1991 would be a season in which Reynard rechallenged Ralt's supremacy with a 913 driven by Barrichello's GM Euroseries sparring partner Gil de Ferran, with TOM's Toyota and Bowman also adding their weight to Ralt's opposition. But coincidentally (or via the same logical thought process that Bennetts had employed) Barrichello's main rival would also have a Ralt-Mugen. His name was David Coulthard, driving for the Paul Stewart Racing team run by fellow Scot Jackie Stewart's son.

Pre-season testing can often be misleading when it comes to predicting likely form, because people can do all sorts of things to their cars when they are allowed to run them in any configuration they want to in testing. Some deliberately run under weight, perhaps in a belated attempt to attract sponsorship, others run lighter fuel loads while aiming purely for fast lap times, while their rivals run more fuel as they try to learn more about their cars' behaviour in race trim. Throughout the early months of the new season, however, Barrichello stamped his mark on testing, setting fastest times wherever he went. It was inevitable that he would start the season favourite, given West Surrey Racing's pedigree and his abundant speed, and observers were quick to appreciate the sheer artistry of his smooth driving. Barrichello looked very much like the real thing.

The British Formula Three Championship is always a frenetic, highly competitive series, with 17 races at a variety of British circuits. It has long been the yardstick by which upcoming young drivers around the world are judged, and many of its past champions and challengers have graduated to Formula One. Title winners Nelson Piquet, Jonathan Palmer, Tommy Byrne, Ayrton Senna, Johnny Dumfries, Mauricio Gugelmin, Johnny Herbert, JJ Lehto, and Mika Häkkinen, together with Nigel Mansell, Martin Brundle, Damon Hill, Martin Donnelly, Mark Blundell, David Brabham, and Mika Salo would all make it through to the big league. Barrichello knew that Arisco's backing, and the resultant alliance with West Surrey Racing, had given him the best possible chance of joining them. On the downside, however, there was also the pressure that accompanied that level of expectation.

The season opened on the Silverstone Club circuit in March, where Barrichello confidently put his Ralt on pole position, as expected. But the race proved a disaster as he stalled on the grid and failed to finish. He didn't even make it to Copse, the first corner. An unexpected victory instead fell to the Swedish driver Rickard Rydell driving the TOM's Toyota, who also set the fastest lap.

Barrichello took pole position again at Thruxton in April, and again he fluffed his start. But this time he recovered to score a resounding victory over teammate Jordi Gene and Rydell, and to set the fastest lap. After the initial hiccough, his campaign was under way, even if Rydell was leading the championship.

The third race, at Donington Park, saw Rydell take pole and David Coulthard add to his fourth place at Silverstone with a superb victory that pushed him ahead of Barrichello in the championship chase, eight points adrift of the Swede. Once again, Barrichello failed to finish.

By now it was clear that, although the Brazilian was an artist at the wheel, he had a problem starting races. Coulthard, by contrast, at this stage had trouble achieving the perfect 'qualifying' lap. In qualifying, the drivers had to use the same sort of tyres on which they would race, but there were ways in which cars could be optimised around brand new tyres and PSR and Coulthard failed initially to achieve them. But unlike Barrichello, Coulthard had a brilliant ability to get his car off the line, almost as if an innate early warning system told him a fraction before his rivals when the starting lights would blink from red to green. On the Brands Hatch GP circuit for the fourth race, the Scot narrowly beat Rydell and Barrichello. De Ferran then won on the Brands Hatch Indy circuit, with Coulthard second and Barrichello only fourth. Barrichello beat Coulthard next time out, at Thruxton, but had to settle for second place behind Ralt driver Steve Robertson, who today manages Kimi Räikkönen's career and started up his own F3 team with the Finn for the 2005 season.

Barrichello was still qualifying well, having started from pole at Thruxton, and he did so again at Silverstone Club in June, but Coulthard scored his third win of the season there to head Barrichello home by seven seconds. Now both had moved ahead of Rydell, to hold the first and second places in the title race; but at this stage the Scot was looking stronger.

Later that month the circus returned to Donington, and there Barrichello turned the tables with a dominant win from pole position, but only after Coulthard had led on the opening lap before retiring. There was a third race that month, and back at Silverstone Club Barrichello could manage only fifth as de Ferran won again. The only consolation was that Coulthard finished only seventh and thus failed to score. Having equalled the Scot's 40 points at Donington, Barrichello now led the championship at last with 42.

The circus stayed at Silverstone in mid-July for the prestigious race that supported the British GP on the long circuit, but the race was a disaster for Barrichello. De Ferran won for the third time, Coulthard was a lowly sixth, and all Barrichello had to show was fastest lap. He still had a two-point lead over Coulthard, 43 to 41, but on 37 de Ferran was coming up fast.

The series paid a visit to Snetterton in Norfolk at the beginning of August, and there, despite setting fastest lap, Barrichello could only manage fourth place as Coulthard scored his fourth victory and grabbed the lead of the series with 50 points to his 46. Worse still, West Surrey Racing teammate Gene finished ahead of him in third place.

Another dismal result followed, with only fifth place back at Silverstone Club, where Japanese driver Hideki Noda headed home de Ferran and Coulthard. On the Brands Hatch GP circuit in September Barrichello managed a little damage limitation as Coulthard won, by finishing third with fastest lap behind de Ferran. But now the title points scores read Coulthard 63, Barrichello 53, and de Ferran 51, and there were only three races left. It was time for Barrichello to pull something special out of the bag if he was to become champion.

In September at Donington Park, he started from pole and set fastest lap on his way to a great triumph, and in October at Silverstone GP he repeated the feat precisely. Both races were a nightmare for Coulthard, who finished fourth after a first-lap incident at Donington, and then failed to make it home at Silverstone when his engine's ECU failed. Suddenly, against the odds, Barrichello was leading the series as they headed into the final race, at Thruxton. The Brazilian had 73 points, the Scot 66, and the latter needed to win with Barrichello fourth or lower in order to beat him to the crown. As it turned out, Coulthard damaged a front wing challenging Noda for second place at the Thruxton chicane, and fifth place was sufficient for Barrichello (who started from pole) to win the title with 74 points to Coulthard's 66. De Ferran was third with 54 after his challenge also faltered through mechanical unreliability in the final races.

So far, Barrichello was neatly following Senna's wheeltracks, repeating the older Brazilian's 1983 success for the team and also handing it its first back-to-back title after Mika Häkkinen had won it in 1990.

'We had nine poles that year,' Bennetts remembered. 'That should have led to nine race wins. We had five. Rubens stalled at the start of the first race and he lost a bit of confidence after that. He started being a bit careful at the starts and a bit cautious on the opening lap. We even took him to Santa Pod to try and sort out the starting problem. He had all three poles at Thruxton, and always lost ground on the first lap. At the final round where he needed only fifth place to secure the title, he came round eighth at the end of the first lap. I took the mickey out of him afterwards and suggested he'd only done it to be sure of the television coverage; he just laughed.

'It's difficult to compare him with Ayrton or Mika. Ayrton was Ayrton. I think that Mika had more outright talent than Rubens; he'd have driven a three-wheeled car if that was how he could win. But I don't want to sound unfair or as if I'm knocking Rubens, because when he came to us he was 17 and he left an 18-year-old Formula Three champion. It helped him that he had a car that was an evolution of the one that Mika drove the previous year, so there was no major development programme to distract him, and the team always knew where it wanted to go with the car. What impressed me with Rubens was the way that he worked with the team. This was in the days before computers. We had a Stack system on the dashboard that told you your lap time, but he had to work together with the engineers to dial the car in and his technical feedback and communication were excellent. And generally he kept himself out of mischief, kept the car out of the weeds.

'He was disappointing at Macau, where Jordi rose to the occasion and beat overall winner Coulthard to take the second heat and finished second overall. Jordi had just found that he had lost Marlboro as his sponsor and had to be really hungry; I think Rubens was on a bit of a cruise there because he already had a Formula 3000 contract in his pocket. He had nothing to prove, whereas Jordi had everything to prove.'

The sceptics, however, were not fully convinced about Barrichello. Some felt he had made his task an awful lot harder than it should have been, with all those poor starts. Others felt that, though he undoubtedly had an artistic touch at the wheel which manifested itself in his silky smooth handling of the Ralt, he was another driver in the mould of Gugelmin, who lacked pure tiger in a tough situation.

Coulthard, unsurprisingly, felt *he* should have been the champion, claiming that Barrichello had only actually beaten him fair and square on one occasion.

'The season was made up of him having a lot of good qualifying and a lot of shit starts, and me qualifying badly and making good starts,' the Scot recalled. 'The season ended with me having five British victories and he had four, and in terms of the year I won the Zandvoort Masters race and I won Macau, so in my opinion looking at the year as a whole I was the most rounded guy. But you would say he had speed but lacked racing experience. It came down to the last race, at Thruxton, and I ran into the back of Noda when I was in front of Rubens and all I needed to do was win to be champion. But at the second last race, at Silverstone, the black box failed going off the line. At the race at Donington in June I was leading on the first lap and it jammed between gears, one of those things that had never happened before. There were three selectors and somehow one of the fingers got jammed between two of them and I got stuck in second. I was bloody unlucky at times in my career!'

Overall, Coulthard felt that Barrichello was a clean opponent, but he remembered a couple of incidents that characterised their tough battle.

'We ran into each other a few times, and we crashed together famously at Silverstone. Rubens will remember this story! After the race my Grandad door-stepped him, because we'd banged wheels, Rubens had got a puncture and I'd got knocked off. My Grandad, Jimmy Marshall, is a big fat man, and he has this broad Scottish accent and doesn't wear his teeth very often because he doesn't like them. He doesn't say "fucking"; instead he says "pucking". So he gets hold of Rubens and says, "You're a great driver, there's no pucking need to do that," at least, that's the general translation. Rubens has always remembered that, the day my Grandad gave him a bollocking.'

'I do remember it,' Barrichello admits, 'but I don't believe the incident with David was my fault!'

The two other major races of the F3 season were the non-championship Marlboro Masters at Zandvoort, and the FIA F3 World Cup in the former Portuguese colony of Macau. Both were open to drivers from all national championships, and were thus regarded as the jewels in F3's crown.

Coulthard won both races, with Barrichello sixth in Holland and fifth in Macau. The Dutch race perfectly captured the difference in their respective styles. Since each national championship runs on different tyres, everyone had to run at Zandvoort on unfamiliar rubber from the GM Euroseries in which Barrichello had competed the previous season. This afforded less grip than the usual Avon tyres used in the British series, but nevertheless Barrichello rose brilliantly to the occasion to snatch a smooth pole position, minimising the negative aspects of the tyres and making far better use of them with his smooth style than anyone else could manage. In the race, however, Coulthard, made another of his blinding starts and nobody saw which way he went. Barrichello, by contrast, overdrove trying to make up for yet another poor getaway, and finished well back after running off track a couple of times.

That was why there were still question marks over his ultimate talent as the season drew to a close. That, and the fact that some of the lap records set by Mika Häkkinen and Mika Salo during their great scrap in 1990 remained unbroken in 1991, even though the latest cars were quicker.

None of this bothered Barrichello. As far as he was concerned he had won the crown, and that was all that mattered. He had achieved his goal. And he knew long before 1991 was over exactly what he would be doing in 1992. The Arisco funding made the transition from Formula Three to Formula 3000 a lot easier than it was for drivers such as Coulthard. But in some ways, that seamless path would have its drawbacks.

In the senior category Barrichello would find himself up against a couple of tough Italians, both of whom would succeed where he failed in winning races. One was Luca Badoer, who went on to win the title for Crypton Racing; the other was Emanuele Naspetti, an experienced Formula 3000 'shoe' who would later move to March's ailing Formula One operation. Both would play supporting roles in his career at later dates, but in 1992 they often did a better job than he did.

Barrichello cemented a deal to run with the Il Baronne Rampante, the team set up for the 1991 season by Giuseppe Cipriani and Roberto Trevisan. He took over the seat occupied to such great effect the previous year by Alessandro 'Alex' Zanardi, who had used it as a springboard to Formula One involvements with Jordan and Benetton. The team had been new that year, but had quickly established itself as one of the best, and only a superior blend of fuel had allowed Naspetti, and eventual title winner Christian Fittipaldi, at Pacific Racing, to inch ahead in the closing races.

At the beginning of 1992 the Italian team took delivery of new Reynard 92Ds equipped with John Judd's KV V8 engine, and now everyone had to run on control fuel. Barrichello appeared to have made a sound choice.

Immediately his consistency became apparent. In the opening race at Silverstone on 10 May he finished an impressive second and also set fastest lap, though his day was blighted a little by the identity of the winner, his old West Surrey Racing teammate Jordi Gene, who finished 18 seconds ahead. First time out on the picturesque but tricky street circuit at Pau in southern France in June he took third, coming in behind the experienced Naspetti and German Michael Bartels. Then in Barcelona later that month he repeated the Silverstone result, finishing second to his teammate, the Italian Andrea Montermini, who beat him by 13 seconds. But Barrichello had been the star, scything back through the field after a poor start and breaking the lap record time, and again as he recovered from ninth place on the opening lap. His result in France had been sufficient to push him into joint leadership of the series with Naspetti. Spain made him the clear leader, but then he had to share it again with Naspetti, who finished second to Badoer at Enna where Barrichello had an horrific outing.

The Italian speedbowl has long been renowned for its primitive facilities as drivers speed round a lake that is populated by poisonous snakes. Big accidents there are a fact of life. Over the years some have been spectacular. This time one of then befell Barrichello. Running strongly, he spun in one corner and went backwards into a rescue truck that had come on to the course to retrieve another car that had earlier hit the tyre wall there. By sheer good fortune the Reynard hit the truck's front wheel. A few feet to the other side, and it could have gone right under the flatbed. With the racing driver's insouciance, Barrichello shrugged it off and Il Baronne Rampante headed to the next race, at Hockenheim in Germany, with a rebuilt car and the determination to maintain its series points lead. All Barrichello could do at the track which would ultimately surrender to him his first Grand Prix victory eight years later, however, was sixth place. Badoer, who won from Bartels and Scottish ace Allan McNish, now put a lock on the championship.

At the Nürburgring in August Barrichello was back on the podium, with another strong recovery to third place with fastest lap, but he should have beaten Badoer and his Crypton teammate Bartels who occupied the top steps. Spa-Francorchamps a week later yielded only fifth place after Badoer stopped the race temporarily by crashing heavily, and Montermini eventually grabbed the win. Albacete and Nogaro produced a brace of sixths as Montermini and Badoer took a victory apiece. The final, at Magny-Cours, was won by Frenchman Jean-Marc Gounon in a Lola after Badoer and Montermini collided while fighting for the lead. Barrichello could only muster fifth. Two of the men who were ahead of him would also graduate to F1; one was Frenchman Olivier Panis, who took second, the other Barrichello's old Formula Three sparring partner David Coulthard, who also set fastest lap.

Barrichello finished third in the championship with 27 points, and for a first season it wasn't a bad effort in a highly competitive category in which it is notoriously difficult to be really consistent. But Badoer was also in his first season, running with a team that kept developing its Reynard all through the year, and he finished first with 46 points, comfortably ahead of runner-up Montermini on 34. Compared to Zanardi's 1990 season, in which the Italian had won races and challenged for the title, it was a disappointment.

'Rubens was very young,' recalls his race engineer Roberto Trevisan, who had set up the team with Cipriani and was a key figure. 'He had very quickly climbed his motor racing Mount Olympus, and that was good and bad for him at the same time. Definitely, Senna was the number one driver of the time and the best Brazilian, and in some ways Rubens was the little boy, but there were many eyes upon him. Sometimes it was too much for his age and level of experience. His talent was very impressive. His natural driving was unbelievable. The only problem was when he was under pressure, and even today sometimes that is his limit.

'In the GM Lotus series he was with a winning team and he won races under the eyes of the Formula One people. In Formula Three he was with a winning team, too, and had a proper budget. He did a very good job so the way was open to him and he had the budget for Formula 3000, and he chose Il Baronne Rampante. In the beginning it was fantastic. Montermini had more experience, but Rubens matched him well and went very quick. But it was a strange season. He should have won many races, but he didn't.'

There was one major reason for this: Barrichello's starts. It was Formula Three all over again.

'We tried everything to understand it,' Trevisan continues. 'It was a disaster! But it was not a technical problem. In practice his starts were fine. But it was what happened in those moments before the start. And it wasn't just getting off the line. Sometimes his first movement was okay, but then the first corner would be a problem. He'd finish the first lap eighth or ninth, and then do a fantastic race, overtaking many people and finishing second. Yet on the first lap he'd been 15 seconds behind the leader!'

Barrichello certainly had the speed. He had shown that in Opel Lotus and again in Formula Three and now Formula 3000. But he still hadn't done enough to shake off his reputation as a guy who couldn't handle pressure. Before him, immensely likeable fellow countryman Mauricio Gugelmin had been regarded as a man who could pedal the car very quickly but lacked what it took, perhaps the sheer aggression, to overtake and to win in anything other than ideal circumstances. Rubens was perhaps one who was similarly a great stylist but who could not quite handle ultimate pressure – until he had nothing to lose. 'That was when you saw what he could do,' Trevisan said, 'when he raced like that – Silverstone and Nürburgring were unbelievable races after he had messed up the starts. When there was no pressure, he could do fantastic things. I remember one time we went testing at the Nürburgring in the wet and he was three seconds a lap faster than anyone, consistently. We stopped because it began to snow, but even then he could probably have gone faster still! That's real talent.'

Barrichello himself took a pragmatic view.

'I think the thing that really hurt us that year was the engine situation. Baronne Rampante had lost out the previous year when they couldn't get the best fuel, and Fittipaldi and Naspetti pulled ahead. This time they all had the same fuel, but by the middle of the season it was clear that their Cosworth engines, tuned by Heini Mader in Switzerland, were better than our Judd KVs. The team decided to switch to Cosworths, which was the right thing to do, but that lost us a lot of time at a critical point of the season. While our cars were at the team's factory being converted, Crypton in particular were not only out there testing, testing,

testing, but were also developing their car. In the second part of the season that proved crucial.'

Trevisan added some perspective to that. The switch to Cosworth came about because of politics; Cipriani had aspirations to go to Formula One and succumbed to Cosworth's blandishments. 'It was a political and economical decision, rather than technical, to drop the Judd engine, which was fine. Its power was good and the weight distribution was better than the Cosworth's or the Mugen's. After the switch we had many problems in qualifying and I think Rubens lost concentration and a bit of motivation because of that, and because he knew he had a Formula One deal with Jordan.'

The situation within the team became so unhappy that Trevisan only stayed there for Barrichello's sake, and quit after the last race of the season.

'Maybe Rubens arrived too quick to 3000,' he concluded. 'His driving was unbelievable. In Barcelona he was half a second a lap quicker than Montermini. He could adapt to the car and track conditions very quickly and was potentially the number one. But I think his way through racing was too easy, and he had this mentality not to make mistakes. Okay, when you are a young driver and you make mistakes, everyone will kill you, so it's correct to try to not make them; but he was sometimes so focused on that that he lost many opportunities to show how strong he could be. Possibly that's the same situation he has today at Ferrari. Some days he is unbelievable, others he is so far from Michael. But there is no technical reason for it.

'What I really liked, apart from his personality, was that he really wanted to understand all the aspects of the car, and he liked testing. At that time he was alone in Europe, so he used to hang around the team and was always happy to test and improve the car.'

At the end of the year Barrichello went back to Macau to drive a Ralt RT36 run by Peter Briggs's Edenbridge Racing set-up. It was being sponsored by Teddy Yip of Theodore Racing fame, a big wheel in Macau.

'I was doing the Fuji race after Macau in the same car,' British driver Warren Hughes remembered. 'The deal was Rubens would do Macau because Teddy wanted a name and he'd been doing Formula 3000, and I'd do the other race. We each did a day's testing at Snetterton and Donington Park, first him, then me.'

On both occasions Hughes – one of racing's more underrated talents who would also see off Jacques Villeneuve as a Formula Three teammate in the future, and was racing in Formula Three at that time – went six tenths of a second faster than Barrichello had managed in the same car the previous day.

'I think it was a case of Rubens needing more time to get his head around being back in a Formula Three car after the Formula 3000, and having temporarily lost an element of the finesse you need to get the most from an underpowered car after maybe getting used to throwing the F3000 around,' he said modestly. 'I wouldn't say I got to know him well, and what I did know really came from going out to Macau and hanging out with the team, listening in. But on a personal level he came across as a nice bloke, unaffected, very down to earth and easy to chat to. Every time I've seen him after that, at a circuit somewhere, he'd always come over and pass the time of day.'

Trevisan endorsed that. 'I saw him recently at the Bologna Show. He was on his own and we hadn't seen each other for a long time, but he was just like it had been ten minutes ago. Very friendly. He's a very, very good guy.'

Bennetts added his own similar recollection. 'At the *Autosport* dinner a few years back a mate of mine, who sponsors our liquid refreshment at races, bumped into Rubens. Instead of just saying hi and moving on, Rubens chatted away and they had some photographs taken. I admire someone who can still be like that after years in Formula One.'

'What I do remember was that he smelled of money,' Hughes continued. 'That's the only way I can put it! His manager Geraldo was with him, and there always seemed to be a couple of people around him, going everywhere looking after him. And there were already strong rumours going round about him being on his way to Formula One.'

Neither driver had much fortune in their eastern sojourn. Barrichello finished seventh, Hughes failed to finish his race. But the fact that Barrichello failed to win a race in 1992 didn't matter. Up in the rarefied atmosphere of Formula One several team owners had indeed been keeping an eye on his progress. One of them, Eddie Jordan, was sufficiently impressed by his performances – and the sponsorship he could bring – to make a firm proposal for 1993. The rumours in Macau and Hong Kong were right: the big time beckoned.

Chapter 3

A STAR IN THE MAKING, 1993

Eddie Jordan and Rubens Barrichello agreed terms for the 1993 season on November 26 1992. The Brazilian was only 20 years old, and one of the youngest men ever to sit in a Formula One car. Jordan had kept an eye on him all through his Formula Three and Formula 3000 seasons. Barrichello was another factor in Jordan's team rebuild for 1993, after an appalling season in 1992 when he had signed to use the Yamaha V12 engine which proved a complete failure. First, technical director Gary Anderson came up with the 193, a new car to comply with revised regulations. Then Jordan signed a deal to run engine builder Brian Hart's all-new type 1035 V10, which was light, simple, powerful, and reliable – in all of these departments everything the unloved Yamaha was not.

All of this would cost money, but sweetening the Barrichello deal was a dowry of $2 million from Arisco, the Brazilian food company achieving its long-term aim of helping him into Formula One. Then Jordan had one of those strokes of luck for which he has become famous. Sasol, the state-owned South African oil company, was interested in a Formula One involvement, and the deal all but fell into Jordan's lap at late notice. It was worth $4 million.

Barrichello made a good impression when he tested an interim Jordan 192 at Silverstone late in 1992, but privately there were concerns about his use of the brakes. He was making the usual mistake young drivers graduating to Formula One would make: lifting off too early for corners, then locking the brakes as the car lost downforce. The trick was to take the car deep into a corner and hit the carbon brakes very hard while it was still generating downforce. The problem was still there when the team went to Estoril for a pre-season test, but otherwise Barrichello exuded the confidence of youth. Jordan was pleased with his choice.

The one serious problem was the identity of his partner. It was one thing to have a new hotshoe who clearly had a big future ahead of him, but to get the best results in a season in which Jordan had radically changed its technical set-up, Barrichello needed a strong team leader. Jordan not only had the new car, but also the new Hart V10. That meant that it needed to complement his skills with somebody with the experience and technical knowledge to sort out the car so that the rookie could concentrate purely on learning about the other aspects of his new role.

Unknown to anyone outside the team at the time, Jordan had been talking on and off for weeks with none other than Ayrton Senna, who was playing a clever game of bluff and double bluff with McLaren, for whom he had driven since 1988 and had won his three world championships. Honda had pulled out of racing at the end of 1992, leaving McLaren to search for a new engine partner. There wasn't one. The works Ford HB V8 was being used by contracted partner Benetton, leaving McLaren with the option of using Fords as a customer (a tough comedown for a champion team used to full works backing), or a works effort from Chrysler which had its own V12. McLaren did not rate the latter sufficiently highly, and was forced to plump for the customer Ford. Without Honda's financial support, the team had less money to offer Senna, and unknown to anyone but the Brazilian and team principal Ron Dennis, they began a cat and mouse game with McLaren's sponsors as they tried to raise the shortfall between what Senna wanted and what McLaren could afford to pay. This would actually go on long into the 1993 season, as Senna continually suggested that he might not do the next race, prompting the sponsors to dig ever deeper into their pockets.

While all this was going on, Senna was also hedging his bets just in case McLaren failed to come up with a technical arrangement that he felt would give him the chance to win races. One of his options was Jordan. On the face of it that might have seemed ludicrous, given that the team had scored but a single point in a disastrous 1992 season with the Yamaha V12 and was only entering its third season. But there were factors in its favour. Senna knew that Gary Anderson's 191 had been the best handling chassis of 1991, and he also had a lot of time for engine designer Brian Hart, having worked with him in his own debut season with Toleman in 1984. It was an outside bet, but the point was that the triple champion was speaking with Jordan, and was treating the opportunity seriously. The combination of Senna and Barrichello would have been excellent.

As long as the chance of Senna signing remained open, Jordan could not identify Barrichello's team leader. In the wings, however, stood Martin Brundle, a favourite with the team after his great Formula Three season with Eddie Jordan Racing battling Senna in 1983. The 33-year-old Englishman had all the resource and experience the team needed, but then he signed instead for Ligier just as Senna finally recommitted on a race-by-race basis to McLaren. Senna's move had been expected, Brundle's had not. So now Jordan was left to cast around for a replacement, and finally its choice fell on Ivan Capelli, a 29-year-old Italian who had worked with Jordan commercial director Ian Phillips in their days together at March/Leyton House in the late 1980s. On paper Capelli fitted the bill perfectly, though his season with Jean Alesi at Ferrari in 1992 had been a total disaster. Phillips believed he knew what was needed to restore Capelli's motivation, and he certainly had the necessary experience. He was confirmed as team leader on 31 January.

In February the team went back to Estoril for further testing, in which Barrichello comfortably outpaced Capelli as the latter played his way back in but, worryingly, the Jordan 193 was almost four seconds slower than the dominant Williams Renaults.

Rubens Barrichello made his Grand Prix debut at Kyalami in South Africa on 14 March 1993. Capelli was slightly faster than him on the first day, but Barrichello qualified 14th, Capelli 18th. In the circumstances it was a reasonable performance.

In the race Barrichello sprinted up to 11th place at the start, but lost his three gained places immediately when he had to take action to avoid Damon Hill's spinning Williams. While Capelli crashed heavily on the third lap, wrecking his car, Barrichello climbed to seventh by the 31st lap, taking full advantage of retirements and accidents. But just as the possibility of points in his first race loomed on the horizon, his gearbox failed.

Brazil brought a similar result as he raced for the first time before his adoring countrymen. The pressure of racing at home could have bowed a less confident driver, but even at 20 Barrichello handled it all with impressive aplomb, even when he lost a lot of time with another gearbox gremlin on Friday morning. Then his engine failed after he had put on his second set of tyres in qualifying, leaving him only 17th on the grid that afternoon. He improved to 14th again on Saturday, while Capelli failed to qualify. Already, Barrichello had become the de facto team leader.

Once again the young rookie made a good start, running 13th at the end of the opening lap and gradually moving up to join the fight for ninth place. Then the gearbox failed again.

By the next race – the new Grand Prix of Europe that marked the only time that developer Tom Wheatcroft's Donington Park circuit in Leicestershire would be used for a modern Grand Prix – Barrichello had a new partner. Capelli had voluntarily stood down, and in his place came Thierry Boutsen, a 35-year-old former Williams Renault driver with three grand prix victories to his credit. Barrichello knew Donington well from his Formula Three days, and benefited from a pre-race test session at Silverstone. But while he retained the Jordan's troublesome semi-automatic transmission and used a new rear wing, the Belgian had a manual transmission in the interest of reliability, and the old design of rear wing. On Friday Barrichello aroused considerable interest along the pit lane by setting eighth fastest time, and though he dropped to 12th overall in Saturday's qualifying session he upstaged Boutsen, who was uncomfortable in the cockpit and could not do better than 19th.

'I had no problems at all with the car,' Barrichello beamed. 'Twelfth place is fantastic for me, but to be honest I might have been able to go a little faster still, because I made a mistake on my best lap.'

It did not go unnoticed that his time was only a shade over a second slower than fourth-placed Ayrton Senna.

Race day was marred by heavy rain in the morning, and highly changeable conditions for the event. The track was soaked, then dried, then got soaked again. This was Senna's day of days, as he stormed up from sixth place in the first corner to the lead by the end of the lap, then destroyed his opposition with pluperfect judgement and other-worldly driving in the horrible weather. It was a spellbinding performance as he unstitched the more potent Williams Renault challenge posed by old rival Alain Prost and rookie Damon Hill, and Michael Schumacher's Benetton Ford. But in Senna's wake Barrichello was also putting in a drive that grabbed headlines.

Opting to retain a dry weather set-up on the Jordan, but starting on wet weather tyres, he showed that day that he possessed true long-term potential. Things swung in his favour when Sauber's Heinz-Harald Frentzen, ahead of him on the grid, had to start from the pit lane. Barrichello dispensed with Johnny Herbert's Lotus and Riccardo Patrese's Benetton on the run to Redgate, the first corner. That gave him the room to take the perfect line through the corner and to close up on Gerhard Berger's Ferrari, which he promptly overtook at Old Hairpin. 'There was no time to register that I had overtaken a Ferrari!' he enthused later.

Next to fall was Jean Alesi in the second Ferrari, who lost momentum avoiding the aftermath of a heavy collision between Karl Wendlinger in the other Sauber and Michael Andretti's McLaren.

'I grabbed my chance going into the next corner, but Alesi is always difficult because he brakes so very late! I was braking late too because I didn't want to miss an opportunity like this. My car went a bit sideways and I thought I was going to hit the side of Schumacher's Benetton, which was just in front of us. Fortunately, he saw me and went a little bit wide – and I was able to overtake him, no problem. So now I was fourth!

'I really committed myself and tried very hard. If you had asked me Saturday to pay £1,000 and that would let me be sixth at the end of the first lap, I would have paid you. And here I was fourth, with just Senna, Prost, and Hill ahead of me.'

It was indeed as extraordinary a feat as Senna's in leading, and the two Brazilians went on to be the stars of the show. But where Senna won easily, Barrichello had a bitter disappointment in store just as he seemed on the brink of a podium finish in only his third grand prix.

As the rain eased Barrichello made his first pit stop to switch to dry tyres, dropping only to fifth as everyone did the same thing. He stopped again for wets on lap 28, keeping his place, but then it began to rain again in this extraordinary event. He stopped for slicks on lap 35 as the track began to dry again, but no sooner had he done so than it began to pour again, sending him scurrying back into the pit lane for more wet tyres three laps later. When the track started drying yet again he stayed out until his wets finally began to overheat, necessitating a final stop for more slicks – only to encounter more rain the moment they'd been fitted. A lap later he was in again for wets, yet still maintained fourth place as everyone else was having precisely the same trouble attempting to outguess the English weather at its most capricious.

If aspects of his performance betrayed his inexperience in making decisions about tyres in such difficult conditions, there was nothing remiss about his driving. When Hill made his final pit stop with six laps left, Barrichello found himself in a remarkable third place. It was too good to be true.

That was when the Hart engine simply stopped, with 70 of the 76 laps completed. Later it would transpire that there had been some finger trouble in the camp: the last top-up of fuel had not been done after the morning warm-up session, and the tank had run dry. It was as simple and heartbreaking as that. But if Barrichello was distraught as he rolled to a halt, he was lifted by the spontaneous congratulations that greeted him all along the pit lane as rivals saluted his outstanding effort. Arguably, given the level of experience, he had even outshone Senna, and that one race had been sufficient to exorcise the ghost of Jordan's terrible 1992 season. His stature had changed, too. He was still the new kid, but he had comfortably outpaced another fancied teammate (Boutsen, who had previously won wet races in Canada and Australia, never featured). Signing Barrichello looked like the smartest thing Eddie Jordan had done since putting Michael Schumacher in his car back at Spa in 1991.

The Brazilian was the man of the moment in the paddock at Imola for the San Marino Grand Prix, the next round late in April, but he came down to earth with a bump. After qualifying 13th with some gear selection problems, he collided with fellow countryman Christian Fittipaldi on the first lap, puncturing his Jordan's left rear tyre. After delays crawling to the pits for a replacement, he was making up ground when he made his first serious error of the season and spun into retirement in a gravel bed. He spun again in practice in Barcelona for the Spanish Grand Prix, as he struggled with more gearbox problems and track conditions that were so changeable his car went from feeling 'really good' in the morning to oversteering in qualifying even though the mechanics had not touched anything. He qualified only 17th, but Boutsen was 21st and the telemetry showed that the Brazilian was getting on the power out of corners significantly sooner than the Belgian.

The team desperately needed some points, but as Boutsen brought his 193 home 11th Barrichello lost ninth place with 15 laps left. He was fending off a challenging Mark Blundell in a Ligier when his Jordan's left front wing broke. After pitting for a new nose he recovered to 12th, bitterly disappointed to see Berger bring his Ferrari home sixth after catching and passing Blundell right at the end. 'I felt that I could have kept Gerhard at bay,' Barrichello admitted. 'I should have scored the final point today.'

Monaco also failed to yield anything tangible. Barrichello's weekend got off to a poor start, just at the very point where he most needed to learn a difficult and unfamiliar circuit. The throttle jammed open and he was lucky to be able to pull of at Ste Devote, the first corner. When he did get going, however, his skill showed through as a rain shower soaked the track and he set the fifth fastest time when the weather was at its worst. Later that day Senna helped him out by showing him the way round for several laps, enabling him to set the 12th best time. He dropped to 16th the following day, troubled by understeer on a dry road that would probably have been dialled out without the problems on Thursday morning.

The following day the Formula One community arranged a little surprise for him. It was 23 May, his 21st birthday, and as he emerged from the drivers' meeting that morning the public address system played him a special Latino version of Happy Birthday penned and recorded by F1 super-aficionado and rock star Chris Rea, a close friend of the Jordan team. Similar sentiments were displayed on the large diamond screens around the circuit. He shared a celebratory cake with father Rubens and team owner Gerard Larrousse, who also enjoyed the same date of birth.

There was, however, no present for him in another frustrating outing. After taking it easy in the first part of the race he lost out to Fittipaldi as his tyres began to go off, complaining when he finally stopped for replacements that the team should have brought him in ten laps earlier. The Jordan might have proved reliable again, but a ninth place finish was tough to take after Fittipaldi went on to take fifth and two more points in a less competitive Minardi.

After brake problems spoiled his qualifying for the Canadian Grand Prix in Montreal, and the race ended when the Hart engine stopped after 11 laps, Jordan reached crisis point. The following race, the French GP at Magny-Cours, marked the mid-point of the season, and the cut-off stage at which travel concessions for the teams were recalculated. The team's last point had been scored in Australia at the end of the previous season, and if it failed to add more points in France, it would lose concessions worth $2 million. Everyone was under huge pressure as they travelled to the circuit in middle France, but a three-day test session at Silverstone, in advance of the imminent British GP, had given them all cause for optimism. They'd gone back to basics, and as a result had learned a lot about the 193. Only Boutsen seemed to remain unhappy.

In France Barrichello really rose to the occasion, qualifying his car eighth as Boutsen struggled round to 20th. The tensions were running higher than ever just before the start, for a fourth row grid position – Barrichello's best so far – could easily lead to points at last. And as the race progressed, Barrichello seemed destined to score at least one. After 35 laps he was running sixth and looking good, but gradually he began to feel the brakes losing their edge. The Adelaide Hairpin after the first couple of corners places huge braking demands on cars at Magny-Cours, and lap by lap the Jordan was increasingly unable to meet them. Immediately behind Barrichello, Frenchman Erik Comas was steadily closing in, but of greater concern was American Michael Andretti, working his way up from the back of the grid in his McLaren and driving the best race of his brief and unfulfilled Formula One career. As Barrichello was obliged to pump the brake pedal on the straights to prevent it dipping almost to the bulkhead when he needed to use it seriously, Andretti began closing in. Hearts were in mouths in the Jordan camp. On lap 65 of the scheduled 72 Andretti gobbled up Comas's Larrousse, and set after the Jordan. At the start of the very last lap the American passed the powerless Brazilian in sight of the Jordan pit, in one of the most crushing moments of the team's season. Jordan and his men were devastated, especially when it transpired that Barrichello's brake problem had been caused by the one-in-a-thousand chance of corrosion inside the copper pipe connecting the brake master cylinder to its fluid reservoir.

There was nothing to cheer on their home ground at Silverstone, either, for the British GP. Barrichello qualified 15th and enjoyed himself fighting with Fittipaldi and Alesi over ninth place in the early laps. 'It was like doing qualifying laps every time,' he beamed. But he could only manage tenth place at the finish, with the clear inference that the Jordan Hart 193 was not quick enough. Boutsen, 11th in France, qualified 23rd and retired with a faulty wheel bearing after 45 laps.

Friday at Hockenheim brought Barrichello his first major shunt in a Formula One car when he slid off the road in the Stadium section at the end of the lap. Slightly abashed, he qualified only 17th, and was up to 12th in the race when a wheel bearing failed. Boutsen never featured in qualifying, lining up 24th, and finished the race 13th.

Hockenheim was important for other reasons, however, for Barrichello and Jordan agreed terms for their future. This was important for both parties, not the least Jordan as Flavio Briatore of Benetton was threatening to steal away Jordan's driver the way he had poached Michael Schumacher two years earlier. Jordan had issued a press release at Silverstone confirming that Barrichello intended to stay with the team. Now, on the evening after the German race, Jordan, the Barrichellos, father and son, and Rubens's manager Geraldo Rodrigues, agreed terms for 1994 with an option for 1995. Once again Arisco provided a dowry. A Benetton deal had attractions, but everyone agreed that it was better for Barrichello to stay where he was for at least another season, and to learn the ropes without the elevated pressure that would surely be an integral part of any deal with a major front-running team.

It was at the Hungaroring that veteran Derek Warwick observed wistfully of Rubens Barrichello, 'I don't know, these bloody young drivers. They're nearly getting young enough to be my kids,' whereupon somebody told him: 'Actually, if you had been a precocious child yourself, Delboy, he already could be.'

Barrichello's youth was not lost on Eddie Jordan, either. Up until now he had had an easy time ranged against teammates such as Ivan Capelli and Thierry Boutsen, who were nearing the end of their careers. Capelli had never really got back into the swing of things as he joined the team at late notice, and never remotely looked like the man who had led the 1988 Portuguese GP at Estoril for Leyton House, or caught both McLaren Hondas the same year at Suzuka. Boutsen had joined up at even later notice, and only after a lot of haggling. Indeed, at one stage Jordan had been ready to sign either David Coulthard or Emanuele Naspetti if the Belgian finally decided against taking up the offer of the drive. Now as he looked forward to 1994, he was thinking of likely lads such as the German Heinz-Harald Frentzen, the promising Finn JJ Lehto, or even older hands such as Martin Brundle or Johnny Herbert, who also already knew the team well. In the end Boutsen stayed until his home race, which followed the Hungarian GP.

In Budapest Barrichello started 16th (15th after polesitter Alain Prost stalled and had to start from the back), but retired on the first lap after hitting Aguri Suzuki's Footwork and tearing off his Jordan's right front wheel going into the top chicane. Boutsen, starting yet again from the back, finished a lacklustre ninth. At Spa, on his home ground and the most challenging track on the calendar, the Belgian hoped desperately for an upturn in fortune, but all he got was further misery. Barrichello underlined his mettle by setting ninth fastest time on Friday morning, but later the tension within the team surfaced as he was accused of not using his second set of qualifying tyres to best effect. The team felt it was his inexperience showing through; Barrichello disagreed. The following day he improved only one place, to qualify 13th, but everyone loved him again after he had sliced his time down to 1m 51.7s. 'It was an unbelievable lap, probably one of the best in my career!' Barrichello suggested with his usual huge smile. 'I thought I could go a bit quicker than yesterday, but nothing near that much faster. I felt like I was setting record laps through every corner!' Boutsen, a desperate 20th, knew he had neared the end of the Formula One road. It came within half a lap of the start of the race, when he burned out his clutch. Barrichello went further, and was running 11th when he suffered another rear wheel bearing failure.

Now, amid anger at the bearing failures, Jordan began pushing ever harder for results. Boutsen had finally quit after the frustration at Spa, and the team began looking towards younger second drivers for the rest of the season. Money was tight, so they had to bring some funding with them, though when it suited him Jordan was happy to confirm that he had paid off most of his long-standing debts from 1991. The two men he had his eye on for the immediate future were both Italian and both raced in F3000: Marco Apicella and Emanuele Naspetti. Apicella would do Monza while Naspetti, who had previous experience in Formula One with Leyton House and was Jordan's official test driver, curiously turned down the chance to run there and elected instead to race in Portugal, as Apicella had a clashing commitment in Japan. Apicella is regarded by some seasoned observers today as one of those talents that somehow got away, a man who deserved better from Formula One. Naspetti, too, was no slouch. But it was tricky for both F3000 stars, slotting into one-off drives, and neither made much of an impression as Barrichello retained the upper hand.

Things started well for Apicella, however, as he went very quickly during a preliminary test at Imola, a track he knew very well. Jordan himself raved about the Bolognese driver's performance there, and had very high hopes for him, but it says even more about Barrichello that he was one of the first to call his boss and tell him how well he thought his new teammate was going. This was the genuine thing, too, not just one driver indulging in a bit of psychological patronising. It's small wonder that the Brazilian has always been liked by his team partners.

At Monza, things eventually went Barrichello's way rather than Apicella's, but not to begin with. On Friday the Brazilian had problems with his traction control and a spin in the second Lesmo corner, a very fast right-hander. He ended the day only 25th, his usual sunny humour absent. The one thing in Barrichello's favour that day was that Apicella had also gone off the road, in the same place.

The Jordan 193 was a tricky car to drive on the limit. Barrichello largely managed the trick, whereas Capelli and Boutsen were long past the stage of their careers where they were prepared to risk everything just to save a few tenths of a second. The following day Barrichello qualified 19th, hampered by the need to switch to the spare car, then a damp track and another driver's engine failure (Lehto's Sauber blew its Mercedes engine right in front of him). Apicella barely got going and ended up only 23rd, strongly criticising the quirkiness of the car's handling and its lack of downforce. In the race they both retired. And they both did so in the first corner, where the high-speed dash from the start-line leads into the funnel of the first chicane. Apicella and Barrichello were both victims of misjudgements by other drivers.

There was, however, a silver lining from the Italian Grand Prix. In his comments about the handling of the car Apicella had been insistent that it needed a longer wheelbase. Gary Anderson said he'd wanted to do that when the car was drawn out and that finance had prevented it; it was in the CAD system when the Italian made his remarks. The change was ready for Portugal, where Naspetti stepped into Apicella's longer wheelbase car. But he could not improve on his fellow countryman's result of 23rd place on the grid at Monza, and Barrichello was only 15th. Little seemed to have changed after all. But Naspetti had liked the improvement in the car during his first test with it at Silverstone, and now Barrichello raved about it at Estoril. 'All of a sudden it had lost its nervousness at the rear end and felt much more forgiving to drive,' he enthused.

There was little to enthuse about in the race, however. Barrichello lost a lot of time creeping back to the pits with a puncture, and finished a distant 13th. Naspetti's engine blew up.

The team stayed on to test in Estoril prior to Suzuka. Anderson was delighted to see Barrichello lapping quicker than he had in the race, and others failing to do so even though conditions were generally better. But the cynics pointed out that Barrichello was chasing fellow countryman Christian Fittipaldi at the time, opening up an increasingly debated suggestion that he was only truly motivated when he had to counter a direct attack from world champion Emerson Fittipaldi's nephew. There was another reason for the test: to give yet another new driver his chance to acclimatise to the car. His name was Eddie Irvine.

Jordan was not short of suitors for the second seat. Capelli had promised £750,000 worth of sponsorship, which dematerialised as soon as he quit. Boutsen brought nothing, but was paid a feeble £75,000 until he, too, threw in the towel. Both Apicella and Naspetti brought sponsorship, around $60,000 and $50,000 respectively. Irvine was different. Unlike other hopefuls, he was doing very well financially racing in Japan, while simultaneously playing the stock market. His earnings comfortably eclipsed many of those mid-way up the Formula One ladder. Irvine and Jordan knew each other well, of course, as Irvine had driven for Eddie Jordan Racing in F3 and F3000. Their partnership had culminated in Irvine's F3000 victory at Hockenheim in 1990, before Irvine's career hit a brick wall and he headed instead for the rich F3000 pastures of Japan's domestic series. In fact, Jordan had wanted Irvine as the immediate replacement for Boutsen, but the Ulsterman's commitments had prevented him from joining the team sooner and in any case he had no intention of paying for the drive (though Japanese fuel company Cosmo was prepared to pay $150,000 for him to drive in the last two races). That was the thing about Irvine. He had so much self-confidence that he seemed arrogant, but in reality what he really had was a fair idea of where he fitted into the Formula One milieu and the balls to communicate it to anyone who was interested.

Jordan secretly liked that, for he and Irvine were of similar character. Moreover, Jordan knew that Barrichello had been losing momentum as the season progressed. He had the speed and the car control and commitment to race in Formula One, but he was still inexperienced. Those who worked closely with him noticed in the second half of the year that his usual sunny disposition was less apparent than it had been in the first half, as the strain of a pointless season, and the burden of leading the team's driving force, weighed heavily upon him. It was a massive load for a 21-year-old to bear, even for one clearly as mature in so many respects as Barrichello appeared to be.

There was another matter for concern: it seemed as if the negative aspects of Boutsen's tenancy had begun to affect Barrichello, generating a less effusive mood.

Irvine, Jordan knew, was not the type to dwell on things. He was a get-up-and-go character who would deal with disaster with an insouciant quip and a heavy right foot, and there was a shrewdness in employing him as the perfect foil for the quietening Brazilian. Barrichello, Eddie Jordan had come to realise, needed 'a kick up the arse' for a variety of reasons, and he believed that Irvine was the perfect man to administer it. Just as importantly, he knew Suzuka intimately, whereas Barrichello had only ever seen the difficult and challenging track in photographs. The Brazilian was about to get a shock, and Irvine's performance would put Barrichello's season into a slightly different perspective. It would also raise his game.

As the team headed out to the Far East for the Japanese GP, it had still failed to score a single point despite the promise of Donington all those months ago, and things were becoming even more critical as Eddie Jordan faced the prospect of having to continue into 1994 without the $2 million worth of travel concessions with which he had started 1993. To a small team that had still to establish itself fully, and that was still only just getting over the financial hurdles of its debut year in 1991, that could mean the difference between long-term success and medium-term failure.

It took Irvine only a handful of laps of Suzuka to shake Barrichello rigid, lapping his relatively unfamiliar Jordan fifth fastest. Typically, he told his engineer Tim Wright that it 'handled like a piece of shit compared to my F3000 car round here.' That afternoon, in the first qualifying session, he was unhappy to be 11th, a significant improvement over recent Jordan form. Barrichello, meanwhile, was 19th and struggling. For the first time since he came into Formula One, he had a teammate who seemed to be much quicker than him. He admitted that it was a difficult situation, but said he had largely expected it given Irvine's experience of the demanding track.

What nobody expected, however, was for Irvine to complain twice the following morning that he got held up on quick laps in the Spoon Curve by ... Ayrton Senna! Later Irvine set the fastest time in free practice, further undermining Barrichello. The Brazilian was stung by his teammate's speed and screwed himself up for a quick lap, finishing the session a respectable ninth. But Irvine was suddenly looking like the new star.

Barrichello got one of Brian Hart's special development engines for the final qualifying session. He was lucky to get in a good qualifying lap before Andrea de Cesaris crashed his Tyrrell heavily in the challenging 130R corner and brought out the red flag. But Irvine wasn't worried. As soon as the track was clear again, Irvine put in two faster laps. Barrichello was on his mettle again. On his next run he took the initiative away from Irvine with a lap of 1m 39.8s, just over half a second quicker. But Irvine's response was stunning: 1m 38.9s. He was seventh quickest. Barrichello improved again to 1m 39.4s, eighth fastest. It was a great effort, but it remained upstaged by Irvine. Then Barrichello spun trying to go faster, and dropped down to 12th overall. It was no consolation to him when Derek Warwick finally edged Irvine down to an eighth place start on the grid.

It was a turning point for the young Brazilian who had lived much of the season riding off the back of his superb efforts in Donington, for now there was a negative train of thought in some quarters that several of the team's problems during the season may have emanated more from the level of commitment in the cockpit than they did from problems in the car. The critics suggested that Barrichello had become too comfortable, having only to beat Capelli and then Boutsen to remain the team's top dog. Now, in only two days, Irvine had given him a serious wake-up call.

'Part of the problem was that Eddie knew Suzuka the way I know, for instance, Interlagos,' Barrichello said. 'And I was also struggling to help the team to move forwards while at the same time trying to keep learning all about Formula One. There was a lot of pressure. But, funnily enough, having another quick driver in the team actually took some of the pressure off me, as we eventually started to share the duties I'd had to carry out alone through most of 1993.'

Barrichello won the inter-Jordan race the next day, and endeared himself to the team all over again by taking a strong fifth place and thus scoring the crucial points that Jordan needed to save its financial bacon. But Irvine once again upstaged him even though he finished sixth, one point-scoring place behind. And it was the Ulsterman who snatched the headlines, too.

From the start, Irvine jumped up to fifth place, passing Michael Schumacher and Damon Hill, before dropping back down to eighth as they used their superior power to regain their places, and local hero Aguri Suzuki also powered his low downforce Footwork past. Then it began to rain, shortly after circumstance had helped Irvine back to fifth place as Schumacher crashed into Hill, Suzuki spun off, and Jean Alesi's Ferrari broke its engine. Like Senna, Irvine stayed out as long as he dared on the slick tyres that Formula One cars used back then, and had to stay out longer still as Barrichello was due in for wets on the lap that Irvine finally decided he needed some. But when his own stop came it was comfortably faster than Barrichello's, from beginning to end. It was another point against the Brazilian. Now Barrichello was seventh, and Irvine had dropped to tenth. But when the track began to dry again Barrichello came in sooner than Irvine, who used his circuit experience to the full. But when Senna came up to lap him, Irvine triggered his own launch into international headlines by repassing him almost immediately and holding off the Brazilian's McLaren as he engaged in his own fight with Hill, one of his old Formula Three and Formula 3000 sparring partners. Senna stewed as he was forced to watch Irvine pass Hill into the chicane, only to have the Briton accelerate past again on the exit. Their duel continued until Irvine finally had to pit for slicks, and Senna was not happy.

Now Barrichello was fifth, but the intelligence of his drive had been completely overshadowed by Irvine's audacity and car control. In the closing laps Irvine finally took sixth place after tapping Warwick's Footwork into a spin at the chicane; but it was the aftermath that really catapulted him into the limelight, when Senna stormed down to the Jordan cabin and demanded to know why Irvine had repassed him after being lapped. He became enraged when the cocky Irvine told him it had been because he was driving too slowly, and the incident ended with Senna throwing a punch which knocked Irvine off the desk he was slouched on. The media had a field day.

Meanwhile, in the cockpit of his car Barrichello had reacted with unalloyed Portuguese emotion over the radio as he scored the first world championship points of his career. He couldn't have cared less about Irvine then, or afterwards, for those two points were enough to save Jordan and were a long overdue payback for Donington.

Everyone came back down to earth in the finale, at Adelaide a fortnight later, where Barrichello qualified only 13th and finished

11th in the Australian Grand Prix after prolonged problems with the traction control system, and Irvine crashed out after qualifying only 19th following electronic problems which cost him track time on Friday.

It was important to Barrichello to have put Irvine back in his place, however, for the events of Suzuka had come close to undoing much of the good that he had done in his rookie season. In the cold light of day his race pace had matched Irvine's lap for lap, and for those who wanted to find it there was evidence that what had happened in qualifying had more to do with the Ulsterman's experience of the track. Barrichello thus ended the year with his burgeoning reputation pretty much intact. He had another year to run on his contract with Jordan, and whoever ended up as his teammate would be fast and challenging and would keep him on his toes. 'In retrospect,' he admitted, 'it was just what I wanted.'

Chapter 4

In the shadow
of Senna, 1994

Even hours before the launch of Eddie Jordan's new car early in 1994, Rubens Barrichello had no idea of the identity of his teammate. Over the winter there had been much talk about upcomers Mark Blundell and Jos Verstappen, after talks with Johnny Herbert had finally collapsed when Lotus refused to release him from a long-term contract, and JJ Lehto opted for the second Benetton seat alongside the emergent Michael Schumacher. But then Blundell lost patience and plumped for a ride with Ken Tyrrell's team, and Verstappen, who was actually expected to take a test drive at McLaren, was snaffled away by Flavio Briatore at Benetton at the last moment.

What few followers of Formula One's off-season machinations knew was that Martin Brundle had once again been firmly in the frame. The Englishman was playing a tricky game, holding negotiations with Jordan while (with Jordan's full knowledge) holding out for a drive with McLaren if reigning world champion Alain Prost decided that a McLaren Peugeot wasn't sufficient temptation. Right up until the press conference to launch the 194, on 11 January, Jordan hoped that he would be able to let Brundle surprise the majority of journalists by driving the car through the usual cloud of dry ice. But at the last moment the Briton finally got the nod from McLaren. That put Eddie Irvine firmly back in the reckoning again (Jordan had always been keen to run him again after his performance at Suzuka the previous year), but not in time for Jordan to announce a new partnership at the launch.

Two things were certain, however: Barrichello's place and Jordan's engine choice. Around the time of the Italian GP the previous year there had been great excitement when the Peugeot car company approached Jordan to initiate discussions about engine supply for 1994. Even a decade ago the value of allying with a major manufacturer was obvious, as it could use its financial muscle to speed up research and development and was likely to make some sort of cash contribution to the running of the team. Jordan himself had naturally long been interested in such an arrangement in order to grow his little team, and for a while a deal seemed imminent. But then Ron Dennis and McLaren entered the equation. McLaren had won its first title back in 1974 with Emerson Fittipaldi using proprietary Cosworth V8 engines. James Hunt repeated the feat two years later. Between 1984 and 1986 McLaren, now under Dennis's management and ownership, won three more titles, for Niki Lauda and Alain Prost, using the bespoke TAG Porsche V6 engine that Dennis had commissioned specially. Between 1988 and 1991 the team had again been dominant, with Ayrton Senna, Alain Prost, and Gerhard Berger, using Honda's power units. But when Honda had withdrawn at the end of 1992, McLaren had been forced to get behind Benetton in the queue for Ford Cosworth engines. The idea of continuing without a key alliance was anathema to Dennis even while that was happening, while Peugeot naturally wanted the most illustrious partner it could find. Faced with forming a partnership with either a proven world championship-winning team or a promising but inexperienced outfit, the French needed precious little persuasion to go with the former. The weekend that saw both his cars victims of the first corner at Monza, Jordan also learned that he had missed the boat with Peugeot.

Gary Anderson's new Jordan 194 thus continued to rely on Brian Hart's doughty little V10. Now it had been modified to lower the centre of gravity, and collaboration with Sasol had created a fuel that helped Hart to realise a three per cent power increase. Missing Peugeot was a major disappointment, but neither Jordan nor Anderson had any reservations about continuing with Hart. All his programme really lacked was the financial clout of the major engine makers, and they continued looking for suitable manufacturers to back it financially.

The 194 was a sleek evolution of the longer wheelbase 193, and behind the scene there was a key change in the technical group as American Steve Nichols – formerly of McLaren and Ferrari – joined as chief designer to relieve some of the load that had been carried alone by technical director Anderson since the team began forming in 1990.

Right from the start the 194 showed strong pace in testing, regularly setting very competitive lap times. So much so that cynics harked back to 1991, when a fast run by an underweight 191 at the Paul Ricard circuit in France had helped Jordan to attract 7-Up as a sponsor. However, the form held up as Barrichello's new season started with tremendous promise. He took fourth place in the opening race in Brazil and then scored his first podium finish, third place in the Pacific GP at TI Circuit Aida. Irvine, however, had retired in Brazil after a heavy shunt involving Brundle, Erik Bernard, and Jos Verstappen, and received a three-race ban for his role in it. Former Footwork driver Aguri Suzuki stood in at TI Aida, but Barrichello comfortably saw him off.

'Interlagos and Japan were very good, fantastic,' he remembered with great delight. 'Wonderful races that did fantastic things for my confidence.' In two events he had scored his best-ever results, taking the first in front of his fellow countrymen, and then going one better in Japan.

And then came Imola.

Just as he had the previous year, Barrichello went there with his tail well and truly up. But an even more bruising comedown awaited him as he prepared to go into his first pukka qualifying lap on Friday afternoon and crashed his car so heavily at the Variante Bassa chicane.

He was in good company, as Michael Schumacher had a 360 degree spin there the same afternoon, but the German was luckier. He got away with it completely unscathed. Barrichello ended up in hospital and did not start the race.

'I had to change the words after Imola,' he said, a trifle enigmatically. Sensing the confusion he had caused, he added quickly: 'I'm the kind of person who is sometimes in the middle of nowhere but listening to good music and suddenly I have to go and write something. To me. I like to do this. It's not a crazy thing, but I go there and I write. Because sometimes, later, you go back and read what you've written, and it is enjoyable remembering your thoughts at that moment. Maybe in 1985 there's something that I wrote that I'll still like to be reminded of today.

'When I got to Imola, I wrote that I was 24 hours from my next qualifying session – it was one day before I crashed there. I was very happy: it was nice weather, da dee da. And after the crash I showed my father what I had written, and I said, "Look at that. How bad is it, because 24 hours before I was so happy, and look at me now. Look at my nose."

'And he looked at me with this expression on his face and said: "Why are you not happy? You're living. You're still here. You could have *not* been here."

'So his words and thoughts changed my mind again, because I was thinking badly, negatively, and he pulled me up. This is the kind of counsel I have from him as a father, and that's fantastic really.'

The following day Formula One came face to face with its dark side when the young Austrian rookie Roland Ratzenberger crashed his Simtek heavily at the fast Villeneuve bend and was killed instantly. Most of the drivers – and many of the people in the paddock – had never had to confront fatality in the sport. The last driver to be killed in a Formula One car had been the Italian Elio de Angelis, who died when his Brabham crashed at Paul Ricard during a test there after the Monaco Grand Prix in 1986.

Another day later, on 1 May, during the San Marino Grand Prix, the unthinkable happened. Barrichello's great friend, mentor, and hero Ayrton Senna was killed on the seventh lap after crashing his Williams Renault at the flat-out Tamburello corner. Not since the death of the great champion Jim Clark at Hockenheim in April 1968 had the sport had to face such a bombshell tragedy as the clear leader of the pack was taken. Barrichello was an extraordinarily mature 21-year-old, but that notwithstanding, he was without doubt completely shattered by the latest tragedy.

'Ayrton was the first person I saw when I woke up in the medical centre on the Friday afternoon,' he recalled, 'and all through my career he had given me many kindnesses. First he raced in go-karts for DAP, then when I went to race for them in 1987 he called a guy there and said that I was going to race, so that was the first help. I think my father had called him on that occasion, and we became good friends. I couldn't see him very often in Sao Paulo because he was too busy and it was difficult, but sometimes I would meet him at the New Year. We kept in touch, most often at the track.

'When I went the first time in Monaco, last year, I felt that I had to ask him how to do it on some corners, because I just didn't know. And he helped me with that. He was a good person to me. I think he would like to have seen me winning races as well. But to others he talked about me quite a lot, too. He helped all he could.'

Barrichello remembered a meal with Senna in Adelaide the previous autumn, where he came back to the table after going to the toilet, to find that, without being asked to, Senna had autographed his cap. It was a small thing, but it meant a lot to him. Then there was the set-up of his Jordan on the first day of qualifying there. Barrichello had been the fastest down the long Dequetteville Terrace main straight on Adelaide's streets, reaching 186mph. But it was Senna who set the fastest lap time. Later he sent word to his young compatriot to go and see him at

McLaren, where he counselled him that straightline speed was nowhere near as important at Adelaide as grip in the corners. He didn't have to do that, but the two shared the bond of mentor and pupil.

'Ayrton was very upset by Rubens's accident on the Friday,' Brazilian news presenter Roberto Carini remembered. 'He was one of the first drivers to go and see Rubens afterwards, in the medical centre, and he was clearly upset by it. When he came to give an interview later on, he was in tears. There was no doubt that it had all had a big impact on his mind.'

On the Friday Barrichello was all too aware that his own accident at Imola could have had far more serious consequences, and the days following the ensuing tragedies of Ratzenberger and Senna were dark and difficult as a young man was obliged to come to terms with the harsh facts that his beloved motorsport was not always about happy days and race victories.

'I travelled to England on the Sunday morning because I couldn't race, so I went home to Cambridge. But I could never, ever, ever think that Senna could be hurt. So when I saw him crash, on the television, and even when he moved a little bit in the cockpit, I didn't know whether it was a last sign or not. But with that movement I said to the people I was with, "It's okay, he's okay." Then I saw the blood and I said to myself, "Oh my God, it's something very bad."

'Within half an hour Brazilians were calling me saying that he was dead. I couldn't believe it. Really, it was a massive, massive shock. It was really bad to hear that. And then the funeral…'

All of Brazil came to a standstill as Senna's body was transported to the Murumbi cemetery, his casket carried by peers that included the great Emerson Fittipaldi, who so many years ago had first blazed the trail for young Brazilian drivers; Jackie Stewart; bitter rival turned friend Alain Prost; Gerhard Berger, the man who taught him to laugh; and Nigel Mansell, with whom he had enjoyed so many on-track battles. Barrichello himself, not yet turned 22, felt very young and very vulnerable.

'I was not bad, because I just couldn't believe it,' he confessed. 'If he had not been covered in the coffin, I would have felt very bad. But because I couldn't see him, I never thought at any time in my mind that it was him, you know? I just couldn't believe that.

'I had never been through any kind of experience like that with death before. My grandfather died, but I was so young ... Ayrton's was the first time that I ever went to a funeral.'

And then, because that is the nature of a sport that cannot linger too long with the fallen, no matter what the degree of their greatness, Barrichello had to prepare for his own return to racing at Monaco. He drove a new Jordan 194 at Silverstone, which replaced the car he had crashed at Imola, to get himself back into the rhythm.

'It was really difficult. Doubly difficult, really, because when I came back to drive I had both my crash and Ayrton's death to come to terms with. I went to Silverstone to see all the guys and they said: "You have the whole day to get used to it again." I said: "Okay, thank you." And I put in my mind the thought that I had to get back up to speed in half a lap. I left the pits as mad as possible – but not doing mad things you understand, just because I felt that I had to do it quick. When you fall off the horse, you have to get back on as quick as you can.

'And in four laps I did a better time than I did in the same conditions before that weekend in Imola. After four laps Gary [Anderson] said: "Why are we testing? You're okay!" So that was a fantastic feeling. It helped me to get back.'

Monaco, however, was to be a nightmare. Everywhere he went there were reminders, of Imola, of Senna. 'Everyone would come to me, talking about him. So that made me feel bad, and it got worse and worse and worse.'

The Portuguese Lotus driver Pedro Lamy admitted after the race that he had been very upset during a one minute tribute to Senna and Ratzenberger on the starting grid just before the race, but Barrichello forced himself to feel stronger and stronger in the event. 'I was trying to separate the bad things. I put in my mind the thought that he would like to see me drive and I would like to drive as well, because that was the thing I still loved. So even there I didn't think much, because I had to start and that was that.

'It was strange. When I felt bad was when I was sometimes alone, and for a week I couldn't sleep very well because at night in the dark I would think quite a lot. It's still like that sometimes when you see a picture or something. I still couldn't believe it, you know? But I was much stronger. I could sit in the car without thinking of the bad things and going wild, without crying. They were separate things.'

Through courage and force of character, Barrichello made it through the toughest phase of his career, and it made him a stronger driver. 'But when I'm alone I still feel as bad, because he was such a good driver and such a good person to me.'

His nonetheless unhappy race lasted only 27 laps before his car suffered electrical failure and a different phase of the torment began. Andrea de Cesaris, who had taken over from Irvine's stand-in Aguri Suzuki after TI Aida, had failed miserably at Imola. But now he rose to the occasion to take fourth place after qualifying a place ahead of the detuned Brazilian. It was a small consolation for the depressed team.

Irvine's return in Spain earned him sixth place, but Barrichello retired with engine failure after 39 laps having qualified a brilliant fifth. Canada brought only seventh, once Christian Fittipaldi had been disqualified for being under weight. Then there was another retirement in France after Jean Alesi spun his Ferrari and they collided, before he finished fourth at Silverstone in the British Grand Prix.

He was relieved that since Spain things had picked up again, and the Jordan had become even more promising. Engine builder Brian Hart described Barrichello's performance in final qualifying at Silverstone as 'His best ever. He just kept on improving, which is difficult to do at the best of times. He's definitely maturing. His feedback is good and he's beginning to deliver the goods under pressure.' Barrichello himself remained outwardly unspoiled by his continuing progress, and never missed an opportunity to give credit to the team for the improved performances.

'The Jordan improved quite a lot with the new regulations,' he stressed. 'I think the car feels quite good.

'Last year I learned a lot, of course, but this year I have learned a different type of thing from starting near the front. It makes you look after the tyres, and use less fuel. You can use quite a lot less of everything. But you have to be quick all the time. I could show, like at Magny-Cours, that I was keeping the pace quite a lot with the people in front. I could see on the big board on the start/finish line that Mansell was getting close to me, but at one stage when his tyres were not so good I started opening the gap a little bit.' Indeed, one of the surprises was that after his stops Mansell's Williams Renault did not make any significant inroads into the Sasol car's advantage.

'And I was catching Alesi a little, little bit. That was a very good race … Things are going very well, the car is good. And I'm giving 101 per cent. That's what makes me feel happy, and makes me go to my bed satisfied with myself. From that point of view I'm very pleased with things this year. I'm not here just to be another runner. I want to be here doing well. Not because there are cameras and I want to appear to everyone. I get my satisfaction from my speed. And that's coming quite good with the car that we have, and I have a teammate that's quite good.'

He also admitted what the team had long known: he found it a lot better having a teammate who could match him, who could keep him under pressure.

'You learn more. I mean, when I went to Japan, for example, last year, I was relaxing. It's not much, but you have two tenths in your pocket that you don't pull out. When Eddie went fast it was too late, I wasn't prepared for that. By Adelaide I had two weeks, and I gave it back.'

As Donington in 1993 had showed, and Silverstone more recently, he was also finally shrugging off the tag he had in his

F3000 days as the guy who could qualify well but wasn't that hot on race day. He knew all about the accusation and he understood it and could discuss it without rancour. 'In Formula One you have to be aggressive. You have to have a good car, and be aggressive. That's all Schumacher is. He has a good car and he's aggressive. And more and more I'm learning how to be that. The testing in Formula One is so important. As much as you do, so much you are going to learn. So for me I sometimes have to have a type of car that is different from Irvine, for example. But I'm still looking after the tyres, still looking after the fuel. You're learning all the time. Learning all the time.'

A string of retirements followed, in Germany, Hungary, and Belgium. A multiple start-line collision involving de Cesaris (now at Sauber), Alex Zanardi, Michele Alboreto, Pierluigi Martini, Mika Häkkinen, Mark Blundell, Eddie Irvine, Heinz-Harald Frentzen, and Johnny Herbert also accounted for Barrichello at Hockenheim, where Irvine had marginally outqualified him; at the Hungaroring the same thing happened, except that this time he collided with Irvine (who was again ahead) and Ukyo Katayama; and in Spa he had an accident as his engine faded after 19 laps. But the race in the Hautes Fagnes region had, however, yielded to him the first pole position of his Formula One career as he made the best use of changeable weather conditions. He thus became, at the time, the youngest driver ever to head a Formula One grid at 22. It would not be the last time that his judgement of when to run and when not to would stand him in good stead in qualifying.

He lost the lead within a third of the opening lap to the inevitable Michael Schumacher, who had qualified his Benetton Ford second, but fought hard against Damon Hill and David Coulthard in their more powerful Williams Renaults until his retirement. After those disappointments he got things back on track with fourths in Monza and Estoril, finally outqualifying · Irvine again on the Cascais track.

The Grand Prix of Europe at Jerez saw him qualify an excellent fifth behind Schumacher, Hill, Nigel Mansell (who had replaced

Coulthard at Williams), and Frentzen, but after a strong run he faded to 12th at the finish. Suzuka, too, was frustrating. This time Irvine started ahead of him again, and where the Ulsterman finished fifth (backing fourth place in Jerez) Barrichello retired with gearbox failure.

Only Adelaide remained, for the Australian Grand Prix, and there he rounded out a promising season by taking fourth place, on the same lap as winner Mansell, Gerhard Berger, and Martin Brundle, following the celebrated incident in which Schumacher crashed and then punted arch title rival Damon Hill off as the British driver was set to win the race and the championship.

Barrichello's efforts earned him a decent sixth place in the world championship, and helped Jordan Hart to fifth in the constructors' series, something that delighted both Eddie Jordan and Brian Hart. The engine builder had himself been a Formula Two driver of note in the heady 1960s, and he had a lot of respect for the young Brazilian, just as he had had for Ayrton Senna when Hart's turbocharged four-cylinder engines had powered the Tolemans during Senna's debut season in 1984. He recognised some of Senna's traits in the younger man, not the least of which was that he was his own man. Even in 1993 Hart had said of him: 'He's a guy who knows exactly where he's going.' But would that now embrace donning Senna's mantle for the sake of his traumatised countrymen?

Where Christian Fittipaldi would deny feeling any need to do that, Barrichello had a different view. 'I have a different feeling, because I have a bit of a pressure, sure. But this support, if you put it in the balance, is almost as big as the pressure. That's a very good thing. I don't sit in the car and think: "I have to be the new Senna." I'm doing well, and the people are enjoying that. We lost ten per cent of the people watching TV after Ayrton was killed, but they are coming back. I'm happy with me, with my performance, and I think the future is looking good. The aim right now is to look to another podium.'

Chapter 5

GOING DOWN AT JORDAN, 1995–6

Rubens Barrichello stayed with Jordan for a third season in 1995, and with Irvine staying too the team finally enjoyed a degree of continuity at last, at least where the drivers were concerned. On the engine front it was a different story.

After a year McLaren had ended its alliance with Peugeot and now moved into a long-term partnership with Mercedes-Benz. Peugeot thus found itself back on the market, and harbouring the feeling that it had been used and then ejected when it suited McLaren. 1994 had brought no victories, though towards the end of the season the McLaren MP4/9 was a halfway reasonable car. The team said it lacked horsepower, but rivals suggested that the French V10 was not far off. Either way, when Peugeot came knocking again, with a new three-litre engine to suit revised technical regulations formed in the wake of the Imola tragedies, Jordan didn't need asking twice to throw his doors wide open. The new alliance was exactly what he needed, although tying up with French fuel company Total meant saying a reluctant farewell to Sasol. Jordan now had some solid support, however, so little things like that did not get in the way. Peugeot's arrival enabled Eddie Jordan to strengthen his team's foundations and to plan for the future. It was a timely event and he was delighted.

But the season did not begin well. The Jordan 195 was an attractive little car that handled reasonably well and seemed quite competitive, but it was unreliable. Neither Barrichello nor Irvine finished the opening races, in Brazil and Argentina (Rubens's gearbox broke at home and the engine in Buenos

Aires), and as Barrichello retired in Imola with another gearbox failure Irvine managed only an eighth place finish. The Ulsterman finally scored the team's first points of the season with fifth place in Spain, where he was slightly the faster of the two, while Barrichello was extremely disgruntled not just to be outpaced but to finish only seventh after losing sixth place to Olivier Panis's Ligier on the last lap. 'I don't know what it was,' he lamented, 'but it felt as if there was no throttle.' Monte Carlo brought two further retirements, faster qualifier Irvine with a wheel failure and Barrichello with a sticking throttle. Suddenly his career was floundering.

By now he stood alone as Brazil's great hope, yet he was still in some ways a boy trying to fill a great man's boots in the wake of Ayrton Senna's passing. Yet soon he would become a seasoned professional, the man to whom younger Brazilians such as Riccardo Rosset and Tarso Marques and, more recently, Cristiano da Matta and Felipe Massa looked for the sort of mentoring he himself had received from Senna. Today it is a role he has grown into, and it comes naturally. But back in 1995 it didn't. At Interlagos he had worn a specially designed helmet to commemorate Senna. But that inner feeling of needing to 'replace' Senna made Barrichello's life very difficult in a number of ways.

'For sure, that season I was trying to be something that I wasn't. You think of Brazil and you think of Ayrton. Back then I felt as if tenth on the grid wasn't any good any more because that used to be acceptable for me when Someone was on pole position, doing the job for Brazil. But without him, I felt greater pressure on me to do well for the country.

'In 1995 I wanted to make up for Ayrton's loss. I was always just trying to be in his position and I was not able to be. I would tell myself: "You have to learn more, because you don't have the car, you don't have the potential to do it yet." So it was really bad. When I really tried hard I was overdriving the car, and at the same time I just had problems with the engine, problems with the gearbox … All the time I seemed to be having problems, so that just destroyed my head. Everything appeared to be going wrong.'

But just when he needed it most, along came salvation in the Canadian Grand Prix.

As Jean Alesi celebrated his birthday by winning the only grand prix of his career when Schumacher hit an electronic problem and had to pit for a new steering wheel, Barrichello and Irvine swept home in second and third places respectively. Irvine had yet again been the quicker qualifier, but Barrichello drove a beautiful race to take the best result of his career, finishing 29 seconds behind Alesi's Ferrari and just under five ahead of Irvine. It was also Jordan's best performance to date.

'I needed this result – *we* needed this result – so badly,' Barrichello said, vying with an emotional Alesi to see which of them could be more tearful.

Two weeks later Barrichello scored another point, with sixth place in the French GP, three places ahead of Irvine.

Typically, Barrichello had analysed the situation in which he found himself prior to the breakthrough. 'I still really had that problem that Ayrton wasn't there any more. I ran well in Brazil, but all the time I was thinking, "Where is he? He has to be here for me to do well." If I was finishing sixth it was like a win for me, but if he wasn't there winning, it wasn't going to be good enough. So then I was overdriving, and left-foot braking wasn't for me. Eventually, you know, the telemetry told me that for six or eight races I'd been using the brakes on the straight! My foot was just interfering with the pedal. How could I ever do that? I was telling the team it felt like there was something wrong with the airbox! I just didn't realise that I was doing it, so I was using more fuel and brakes, and nobody saw it for ages on the telemetry!

'It got so bad that at Monaco I told my father, "Don't be afraid, but I'm gonna hurt myself. Because I'm driving better than ever, and the times just aren't there." I was two tenths slower than Eddie in qualifying, and those two tenths were just inside the tunnel. I was faster in every corner, but just in that little straight I was slower because inadvertently I was pushing the brakes.'

When he reverted to right-foot braking, the result was that second place in Canada, and thereafter his career came back on track. 'I qualified right with Eddie and finished second. I outqualified him again at Magny-Cours [he was fifth on the grid] and was close again at Silverstone. It was like bowling; the spare, the strike, and then I was getting there again. You know, so much of this game is in the head ...'

After that flurry, however, it was back to unreliability and frustration once again. In the following grands prix, Barrichello seemed either to retire or to finish out of the points as bad luck struck. At Silverstone he was only 11th after his fight with Mark Blundell for fourth got a little out of hand and the Jordan and the McLaren touched. Barrichello had a hefty shunt. Eddie Jordan was very unhappy at losing another three lucrative points, but not as unhappy as his driver.

'Blundell wasn't fair in his driving,' he fumed. 'Twice he brake-tested me and then, when I came up to overtake, he moved over on me. I am really upset – that's something I would never do.'

Blundell, a tough Englishman who had come up the hard way, lost time but finished fifth. 'Rubens only closed in because Martini held me up for a couple of laps,' he said. 'In the end I defended my line and Rubens hit the back of my car ...'

At Hockenheim Barrichello was fifth on the grid again, just ahead of Irvine, but the engine broke after 20 laps while he believed he was on course for the final podium position; at Hungaroring he finished seventh, after qualifying poorly in 14th place. This was even worse than Spain, because he had driven brilliantly to reach third place and lost it only on the final corner of the final lap when his Peugeot engine cut out. 'I guess it was probably the pneumatic valve actuation,' he suggested glumly. 'It just cut out suddenly, with absolutely no warning.'

Another fine qualifying run (sixth) at Monza ended with clutch failure; at Estoril he started eighth but finished 11th. In

Aida he had a lot of trouble with a new kid called Jan Magnussen who stepped into Häkkinen's McLaren at the last moment when the Finn needed an operation to remove his appendix, but while the Dane finished tenth Barrichello dropped out after 67 laps with electrical failure. In Suzuka he got held up by Irvine, who had set his Jordan up expecting the race to be wet and found to his chagrin that it was dry; as Barrichello tried to squeeze by the understeering Ulsterman at the chicane he outbraked himself into retirement after walloping the outside wall. It was a rare miscue: 'Thank God I didn't end up taking Eddie out as well,' he said after his teammate had taken an eventual fourth place. Finally, in Adelaide, he qualified a sound seventh and, on a two-stop strategy to his teammate's three, was running right behind Irvine after 20 laps. But then Barrichello made another error and ended up sliding out of the race on a day when everyone retired and Olivier Panis brought his ailing Ligier home second to Damon Hill and ahead of Gianni Morbidelli's Arrows.

There were only two real bright spots in the second half of the season. The first came at Spa, where his 195 was reliable enough to take a point for sixth place. Then at the Nürburgring he was fourth, with Irvine sixth. There was an amusing footnote to the latter race when the FIA decided to hold the sport's first drugs tests. Some more gullible members of the media got every excited when two drivers' names came up as testing positive: Rubens Barrichello and the promising Italian Max Papis (two of the last people on earth likely to take drugs). It transpired that both had head colds and the so-called 'hard' substances that were detected in their systems were actually consistent with nothing more harmful than ordinary cold medication. Once each had produced evidence of what they had taken the whole thing was wisely dropped, but not before one tabloid writer had his exclusive 'Drivers on Drugs' story all ready to go.

It had, however, with all the pressures and the unreliability of the Jordan 195 Peugeot, been a trying year. And it was not helped by Irvine's manner. Where Barrichello heaped pressure upon himself, trying to live up to Senna, Irvine appeared far more relaxed. Whether he felt the aggravation but kept it hidden, nobody ever really figured out. Probably not, was the likely answer, for he was laid-back in the extreme, an open and likeable character who exuded self-confidence. Certainly, to the outside world he seemed not to give a damn about anything in particular. Whatever the problems, he rolled with the punches and just kept smiling. If things were beyond his control, why should he worry? That attitude got right under Barrichello's skin, and as soon as Irvine realised that he used it to needle and outpsyche his teammate whenever he could. It was part of the game. On the track, however, Barrichello appeared to have the upper hand, as far as sheer speed was concerned, and Irvine rarely looked like putting one over on him the way he had in Suzuka in 1993.

It was thus to Barrichello's considerable chagrin that it was the Ulsterman to whom Ferrari turned when it needed a new teammate for incoming star Michael Schumacher, as Gerhard Berger and Jean Alesi were pensioned off to Benetton. Ferrari's choice of Irvine was announced at the Grand Prix of Europe at the Nürburgring, after some trading between Eddie Jordan and Ferrari's Jean Todt, and Barrichello regarded it as a slap in the face after all he had done and all the promise he had shown, an indication that he had not been high enough up on the Scuderia's shopping list. It was another blow to his battered morale, but though he had no way of knowing it then, Ferrari would play a key role in *his* future.

'I had to recuperate a lot of the things I had lost on the mental side,' he admitted as he looked back on a season of highs and lows. 'I took my vacations to work out how to enjoy life, because right then I really wasn't enjoying things.'

Deep within him the obsession to live up to his mentor Senna still held him firmly in its grip, but he was gradually getting better control over it. Time, he admitted, eventually gave him the deeper perspective that he needed as he focused on doing everything he could to push his own career forwards.

After the near misses in 1993 and again in 1994, Martin Brundle finally signed a contract to join Eddie Jordan's Formula One team, 13 years after they had together challenged Ayrton Senna for the British Formula Three title in that dramatic 1983 season. Barrichello immediately made the Briton feel welcome, but circumstances in Melbourne, to which the Australian Grand Prix had transferred at the beginning of the season in place of Adelaide at the end, did not. Barrichello qualified eighth as Brundle struggled to 19th spot on the grid, and on the first lap the Briton got into a tangle with fellow countrymen David Coulthard and Johnny Herbert and barrel-rolled dramatically into a gravel trap before running back to take over the spare car for the restart. The ferocity of the accident made everyone in the team feel edgy, and after an adrenaline-charged Brundle had spun out of the new race on the opening lap, Barrichello lasted 29 laps before his Peugeot engine broke.

In Brazil Barrichello shocked everyone by qualifying a stunning second, behind only Damon Hill, and when it poured with rain before the start of the race he was really able to mix it with the big boys for the first time since Donington, three years earlier. In particular he had a great fight with Alesi – the pair frequently swapping places in the first corner – and Schumacher. Indeed, only the unfortunate decision to take a second set of wet tyres in his first pit stop, and the need to stop again for dries nine laps later, had allowed the German, now a Ferrari driver, to take third place. Rubens was pushing along in fourth, way ahead of Irvine in the other Ferrari. It was clear that on this day the Jordan was quicker than the Ferrari, and in his home ground Barrichello had much at stake. Schumacher was a double champion at this point, but had not yet quite assumed the mantle of greatness he enjoys today. Behind them both, leader Hill was about to lap them while fending off a determined challenge from Alesi.

On lap 60 Barrichello pulled off the move everybody wanted to see as he passed Schumacher, only to be repassed immediately on the exit to the tricky downhill corner. Then, as they reached the end of the back straight (where Irvine's accident had happened in 1994), Barrichello lost the Jordan and spun into retirement, his car revolving right across the bows of Hill's approaching Williams. Most observers believed that the Brazilian had simply overcooked things; the man himself suggested that his brakes had overheated during his previous passing attempt and had caught him out.

In Argentina he finally got some points on the board, taking three for a reasonable fourth place from sixth on the grid. To his great pleasure, he was ten seconds ahead of Irvine in the second Ferrari.

The Nürburgring hosted that season's first European race, and there more points awaited the Jordans as Barrichello led Brundle home in fifth and sixth places. Now the Jordan Peugeot package was beginning to run well, and after his shaky start Brundle was beginning to match Barrichello's pace. In fact, Barrichello might even have had a shot at fourth place; after he tried a move on David Coulthard that didn't come off, Hill found the mustard yellow Jordan right on his tail as they took the flag.

There was another fifth place for Barrichello at Imola, this time well behind fourth man Irvine in an improving Ferrari. Monte Carlo and Spain, however, brought two more double retirements. Rubens's sixth on the grid in the Principality was rendered academic by a start-line accident, and Brundle later spun out. In the wet in Barcelona, where Schumacher scored his first-ever win for Ferrari, both cars broke their transmissions.

Barrichello's third consecutive retirement came in Canada thanks to a clutch fault which dogged him from his eighth place on the grid, but Brundle salvaged a point for the increasingly disappointed and frustrated team, having been in contention for fourth until a brush with Portuguese driver Pedro Lamy. After Brundle beat him in qualifying and the race at Magny-Cours during the French Grand Prix, where they finished only eighth and ninth respectively, they both scored some much-needed points again with fourth and sixth places on the team's home ground at Silverstone, Barrichello finishing ahead of Brundle on that occasion as the Briton was delayed by a third stop because of a puncture.

Barrichello added a brace of sixths in Germany and Hungary as Brundle faltered, before both retired again at Spa: Rubens stopped when the handling went awry, and Brundle's Peugeot engine blew.

By now there was a feeling of growing crisis in the team. Jordan was disappointed with its car and Peugeot's engine; Peugeot was disappointed with the 196. Brundle had begun to get on top of his job, but Barrichello appeared to have lost his edge and the cars were losing ground to the opposition. But then came Monza, one of the toughest circuits with its long full-throttle runs, and ironically this time the 196s were reliable again after some hard work from Peugeot. There was a double points finish as Brundle took fourth literally just ahead of Barrichello. But as the Englishman recalled, that was the closest they came to personal aggravation all year.

'I can't remember us ever having any run-ins that we had to clear up. We used to travel together, go to PR things, no problem at all. And still, obviously with the exception of DC [David Coulthard, whom Brundle manages today], probably I'm as close to Rubens of the current drivers as I am to anybody.

'Rubens and I were running very closely in Monza, then the team swapped our pit stops around; they got him in front of me, basically. But he inadvertently switched the engine off as he came out of the pits, He caught the ignition switch, and I got back through again. As I was going around the Curva Grande he kind of had a nibble … Momentarily he turned the wheel my way, but then had a sensible pill and stopped. That would have been nasty. But that was the closest we came to a run-in, really.'

Barrichello, however, was not happy to be beaten by his teammate.

The final two races, in Portugal and Japan, brought no respite. At Estoril he retired after 41 laps when he spun off, and Suzuka brought him an unhappy ninth as Brundle claimed a good fifth, ending his Formula One driving career with a two-point finish.

If Brundle had a relatively happy year, however, Barrichello did not. The Jordan 196 flattered only to deceive. The Peugeot V10 was generally adjudged to have competitive horsepower and Anderson had the same clever ideas about low cockpit aerodynamics as Patrick Head and Adrian Newey at Williams. Straightline speed was excellent, but the cars lacked rear-end downforce and were a handful. Barrichello also found things increasingly difficult as his relationship with the team that had brought him into the big league deteriorated steadily.

Relationships in Formula One are frequently as enduring as they are in Hollywood. Damon Hill's six-year stint at Williams, and Barrichello's four at Jordan, were at that time exceptions rather than rules (David Coulthard and Michael Schumacher were only just beginning their personal respective marathons with McLaren and Ferrari). When things do last so long, however, there is often a feeling of acrimony when they finally come to an end. Certainly Barrichello felt that way as his spell with Jordan drew to its close.

Immediately after qualifying for the Portuguese GP in Estoril he denied that he had signed an option to join Jackie Stewart's nascent Ford-powered Formula One team, which was to be based in Milton Keynes. And at Suzuka he continued to claim that there was still a chance that he might stay with the man who brought him into Formula One, and even suggested that might be his preference. 'There is a chance still with Eddie. For sure they found the problem with the car this year, but it could have been the problem of the last four years. Turn-in oversteer and low-speed mid-corner understeer, and they found the cause in the wind tunnel. For sure next year's car is going to be good. If you ask me would I go over the top of everything to drive next year's car, yes, maybe yes.'

But he had also let the cat out of the bag when he said cuttingly: 'I don't want to say that Eddie is not professional, but Stewart is on a different level.'

In fact, as he spoke he already knew that Jordan had earnestly advised him, at the start of the 'silly season', to take up any options that he had. That was what hurt. After four years, the team no longer wanted him. Jordan was looking at Michael Schumacher's incoming brother, Ralf, and Italian hotshoe Giancarlo Fisichella who had driven for Minardi in 1996. The relationship was over.

'To be very honest with you,' Barrichello continued, when pressed to analyse his options, 'Stewart is the highest one. I see a great future there. Sauber is a good team, I love the way that they do the work. It is very clean. Peter Sauber and Max Welti [then Sauber's team manager] are fantastic, but I don't know what the engine is gonna be, so it's very hard to say something.' Eventually, the Swiss team would cement an engine supply deal with Ferrari, which began in 1997. 'Jackie and I have discussed things, and I am going to England Monday night and stay there Tuesday and Wednesday before I go back to Brazil. By then I think I will have sorted out my future.'

The deal for Rubens Barrichello to join Stewart for 1997 was confirmed the following week.

But what had gone wrong at Jordan? In 1993 the Brazilian Boy Wonder could seemingly do no wrong in his debut season, and in 1994 he'd run strongly, too. Thinking about it all, Barrichello's expressive mouth sagged, and he paused for a long time before eventually the analysis came tumbling forth.

'I was left alone, I was left to one side a little bit since the middle of the year,' he said in a rush.

The period of isolation he described coincided with Jordan grounding chief designer Gary Anderson, who had always been one of Barrichello's staunchest supporters, and getting him to make a head start back in the factory on the 1997 Jordan 197. 'This year my engineer Andrew Green and I did a fantastic job, but even so Gary was there to support me the last two years. After he went away I felt that I was a bit apart, and my problems started then. Martin began to go faster. I never ever said that he had better equipment than me, but I never could actually fine tune the rest of the things like he could. So that was upsetting.

'To be left apart, isolated, was the worst thing for me. If you look at my job, since I came into Formula One, if we go through that door again and you go with me, you know what I can do. You know what you will get with me. Okay, this is a bit of an emotional side, but it counts. So when you hear things going on behind you, behind your back, that isn't very good.'

Gary Anderson remembers it this way: 'Rubens was someone that in his early days of Formula One I really liked as a person and liked working with. I engineered his car in 1993 and 1994 and we built up a really good rapport, which is something that is really important between a driver and his engineer. As Jordan grew a little I had to pass this on to someone else and this never really clicked, so Rubens got really restless and lost a lot of his confidence. Also Irvine became more of a pain if that was possible during 1995, so this also hurt him.'

The history books are crammed with tales of hotshoes who cooled down, and Barrichello was determined he wasn't going to be remembered that way.

'Look, in 1995 and '96 I've been going down. Martin started beating me from the middle of the season, and things just got worse ...'

The endearing thing about Rubens Barrichello has always been his complete honesty, and his unwillingness to hide his inner feelings.

'1996 started well. I qualified second at Interlagos, and found I could race Michael there. It had felt so good in Melbourne when Martin came and asked me could I teach him my lines. An experienced man, asking a boy ... Then halfway through the season he started getting in front of me, and I knew that I was driving flat-out. Then I discovered that our cars were different. I felt that the team let me down ...'

Brundle had started to get a better handle on set-up, and that proved crucial. The desperation Barrichello had been feeling surfaced at Monza, during the Italian Grand Prix, in that near clash with Brundle.

'It was his team when I came in, though it was my old team from Formula Three in 1983,' the Briton recalled. 'But to begin with I had that crash in Melbourne, and then my Dad died, and it was all very difficult to begin with. I had a very difficult three or four months of my life around then, and then I started to get it together and scored my first point at the Nürburgring and from then on I was actually quite strong.

'I enjoyed working with Rubens. He was a straightforward teammate, maybe sometimes a bit emotionally driven in the way that he approached things, but he was fast and reliable and fitted in well.

'We had a full share of all our information. There was never any secrecy. I think once I got up and running, in the second half of the year, I was as quick as him. And we were working hard there at Jordan, it was a solid year. I remember, the first test we did, at Estoril, I did nine days, 900 laps, something absolutely outrageous. And he did a similar amount. A staggering amount of work.'

Doubtless the workload contributed to Barrichello's feeling of depression. Things had deteriorated so much that in Estoril Eddie Jordan was saying some hard things publicly about his young star, and even then was already suggesting openly that neither of his drivers would be staying for 1997 ...

'Jordan brought me very good things, especially bringing me into Formula One,' Barrichello acknowledged. 'But I definitely think that the team is in a position now because of my service as well. They were in a different position when I started. Until 1994 it was very, very good. In 1995 I had all the problems you could have. Pressure, engine breaks, gearbox breaks ...

'Like I did this year, I felt apart, because Eddie started very well in the season, and they didn't give me the support. I had to find that myself. That was why I was so proud, at the end of the year, that I was ahead of Eddie. Then they started to give me the support, because I found the motivation myself.

'Eddie [Jordan] is very supportive when he wants to be, but he is also very depressing when he wants to be. Since the middle of this year, I didn't have that support. Definitely, I didn't have it.'

At the beginning of 1996 insiders at Jordan said Barrichello seemed like a new man after getting his head back together during his winter break. But soon those same people began to complain about him again, and to level accusations about his lack of motivation and to express their unhappiness with the level of his input, particularly on the PR front. Barrichello denied it all, but quite possibly it was simply one of those situations where all of the parties had just been together, without the level of success they sought, a season too long.

'It could be that,' Barrichello conceded. 'It was very, very hard to say what I should be doing. There was no point in saying that I should go just because we have been together four years. Nelson was with Brabham seven years, Mika has been at McLaren in the same situation as me, Panis with Ligier, so I didn't think that way. If I was going, it had to be because I had a problem, or I thought there was a better future elsewhere. But everyone has to be professional, and live with what they have. So even if I didn't have a good car, I had to find the motivation to live with that. So if the team thought that for some reason the driver was the problem … well I don't think it was that way.'

At the beginning of the year Eddie Jordan spouted his usual new car launch platitudes, including the gem: 'There's been too much hype in the past, so this season we are trying to be low key. However, my feeling is that with a little bit of luck we could be third in the constructors' championship. The 1997 season has got to be awesome for us, but in 1996 I consider it essential that we win at least one race.' Given that was his aspiration, 1996 was just desperately disappointing and such expectations, when unrealised, created a situation in which nobody was happy.

'I think we started really, really well,' Barrichello said. 'We had the same car we have now, but we didn't improve as much as the others. They were so far down, so Brazil was very good. Fantastic.

Then there were all kinds of problems and pressures, and the car was in the gravel a lot. If you go back you can say, "Oh yeah, I could have waited a little bit more." But it's passed.

'What makes me feel good in life is that every day you must find motivation. You talk to someone who is 50 and has only worked in offices, their life maybe goes down and down. He has to find motivation to keep it up. The same goes for me. I'm not that 20-year-old boy I was when I started, I'm 24 now. I'm still very much young. But I need to find motivation, to go round all these problems. And it's hard to find when you have had high expectations and then nothing happens.'

Things got so bad that around the time of the Italian GP at Monza in September he actually looked closely at IndyCars, where there was a seat free in Carl Hogan's Penske team. He was adamant that only his manager, Geraldo Rodrigues, spoke with Hogan and that he himself did not get involved, but things went far enough that Eddie Jordan was approached to give his permission for Barrichello to test for the team. In the end, it didn't come to that. 'It wasn't something I would like to do yet,' he admitted. 'I don't have to get old to get there, it was nothing like that. The only thing that I was looking for was to be competitive. I came into Formula One winning everything I could in the past, and I don't want to spend my time here getting nowhere.

'The F1 circus was just not making me feel good. I really do think that my work with Jordan was very good, and I have learned a lot. I had chances to go with other teams in the past and I didn't go, and now they are starting to talk that maybe the driver isn't good. I don't think that at all!'

Eddie Jordan looked back on all this early in 2005, shortly after selling his team to Russian businessman Alex Shnaider, and said: 'You know, I don't remember there being much of a problem in 1995. It was more 1996. I think Rubens always thought that Gary was his saviour, and maybe he felt he had shifted a bit to Irvine. Eddie did his best to undermine Rubens, but then he did that to all his teammates apart from Michael. Hand on heart, I can't really say what went wrong. I think at times Rubens had problems in his management relationship with Geraldo, perhaps because he wrongly thought that Geraldo was closer to the team. I don't know. But in any case, four years is a long relationship in Formula One. And on balance, it was a great four years.

'Look, we are still great pals. Rubens was 19 when he came to me, and he grew up with us. Our families know each other. He knew I wanted him to be a winner, and I would have had him back any time after he left us. He is a sensationally good fellow, absolutely brilliant.'

In the end, the Stewart Grand Prix deal proved too attractive. 'That kind of opportunity doesn't come up every day: the chance to build a new Formula One team from the ground up,' Barrichello said. 'I wouldn't have done it at this stage of my career if I wasn't completely confident in Jackie and Paul.'

For the young Brazilian who idolised Ayrton Senna, Formula One very definitely remained unfinished business.

Chapter 6

TARTAN TERROR:
THE STEWART YEARS, 1997–8

'As far as I'm concerned, Stewart Grand Prix was where my Formula One career started over,' Barrichello claims today, and it was small wonder he felt that way back in 1997, too. Together, he and Jackie and Paul and their tight-knit little team very nearly won their fifth race together – in Monte Carlo, of all places.

As he took stock of his career, particularly whenever he looked back to 1993, he admitted that he might have been looking at a kid brother. 'At Donington I would have finished third, without the problem; that would have been a good podium with Ayrton ... But in 1997 I had to have a different vision. As far as I was concerned, I had to start all over again.'

The mention of Senna inevitably raised the question of whether his cherished memory of the great Brazilian had actually cramped his style since the bad days of 1994 and '95. But while remaining faithful to Senna's memory, he was careful to leave no doubt that it was motivating rather than debilitating. 'It's fallen into perspective now,' he said. 'I'm much more laid-back now. I understand the facts of life. Ayrton had to go, and I understand that now. The fact that he is not there on the racing track is not affecting me any more. And I want to win for myself now, first, before I want to win for Brazil. I'm doing much better on that side. I'm not going now to Brazil believing that I have to deliver for my countrymen. I don't feel angry or depressed with the bad times I've had, and I don't want a payback, but I want to work as hard as I can and not get into that situation where people can ever say that I'm not delivering. I try 100 per cent all the time, and I believe that my time will come. You must have a chance in life where you can prove people wrong. The first time I imagine myself driving a really competitive car, whether it's for Stewart or another team, I hope that people will see what I can do and say, "Whoa, what a waste of time all these bad years have been!"'

As it transpired, Monaco would be the only high point of a bruisingly tough season for the young team.

The Stewarts were adamant that their expectations for their first season as a Grand Prix constructor were modest: 'Upper midfield, in qualifying or racing, would be terrific by the end.'

They faced a mountain. It was a brand new team, and winter testing left precious time for relationships to gel. It did not qualify for any of the FOCA travel concessions, or for any prize money. The Stewarts and their people were minnows swimming among sharks. But when the two Stewart-Fords lined up on the grid for their first race, the Australian Grand Prix in Melbourne's Albert Park in March 1997, Barrichello was an impressive 11th fastest, his teammate – the Danish driver Jan Magnussen, against who he'd raced at Aida two years earlier – 19th. Barrichello's engine broke after 49 laps, but it was a start. They had broken the ice.

He qualified 11th again for his home race, at Interlagos, but this time the suspension broke after 17 laps. In Argentina he collided with Michael Schumacher in the first corner on the opening lap, but he had started from fifth position on the grid, sandwiched between the Schumacher brothers. He loved the Bridgestone tyres which Stewart, together with Alain Prost's team, used in preference to the Goodyears used by the others. While Schumacher retired immediately after what most thought had been an over-enthusiastic overtaking move, Barrichello cleverly used the resultant safety car period to make two pit stops for repairs without losing a lap. Unfortunately, however, his race ended with hydraulic failure after 25 laps. Imola brought similar disappointment when his engine broke after 12 laps.

Then came Monaco.

As a non-FOCA team there was an initial setback when Stewart was not allowed to take up valuable space in the crowded paddock, and instead had to set up shop in a car park that was a 15-minute walk away. But they would have the last laugh. On merit Barrichello qualified an excellent tenth (Magnussen was only 19th), and following a strong start on a wet track he was immediately running with the leaders, in fifth place. Only the Jordans of Giancarlo Fisichella and Ralf Schumacher, and polesitter Heinz-Harald Frentzen's Williams, separated him from leader Michael Schumacher's Ferrari. On lap two he passed Frentzen, and then Schumacher Jnr on lap five. By lap six he had jumped Fisichella, too. Schumacher was 20 seconds ahead, and such was his pace he was clearly going to be uncatchable, but the Stewarts watched in disbelief as their little Brazilian, in their white car with its blue and red tartan stripes, held an easy second place. Two nail-biting hours later, Barrichello was still there, chasing along behind Schumacher. They had scored their first points in style, thanks to Barrichello's super smoothness. Adding to the euphoria, Magnussen was seventh.

The Stewarts later likened the emotion to that which accompanies the birth of a child. 'It would not have been so satisfying if that success had come easily,' Paul Stewart said. 'We'd had a tough time bringing the team together, then Rubens had driven so well and had fought for the position. There was an incredible feeling between my father and I at the end. All I could do was grab his head and kiss and hug him! If we hadn't had the tough time, it wouldn't have been the same. It was so, so intense. It was a fantastic feeling.'

As a beaming Barrichello went to visit Prince Rainier on the podium, Jackie and Paul hugged one another and wept openly. 'You know,' Jackie said, 'I can't account for the emotions that day. Really I can't. When I raced I always tried to control the emotions either in victory or defeat, happiness or even death. I always had very strong control of all of these emotions. I had never been affected in the way that I was then in Monte Carlo. I don't know what it was. It wasn't even the pressure we'd been under, or anything like that.

'I think it was partly to do with Paul, that it was something we had done together, and partly to do with the all the aggravation of getting all the deals together. The result could easily have happened at any race track, but maybe it was the closeness of Monaco that made it so special. There we were, sitting on these wee stone blocks in the pit lane, surrounded by trees, watching a tiny television set. It was primitive almost, not like being up on a pit wall. Maybe it was the intimacy of the two of us having sat there together, rather than being separated on the pit wall ...

'It just meant so much. It was an immensely important moment. And, you know, I was annoyed with myself, weeping like that. Now I just laugh and tell people it was because I had never been second at Monaco. I was third after leading in 1965; after that I either won or retired!'

The former champion summarised his driver's race perfectly: 'Monaco is the jewel in the crown of grand prix motor racing. Rubens drove fantastically well. He really put it together superbly.'

The Brazilian's only error came at the chicane during one lap, but otherwise his was a faultless performance that once again reminded everyone of his potential. But the rest of the season was inevitably an anti-climax after that, and engine failures blighted much of it.

Barrichello suffered one in Spain, another in France, one in qualifying in Britain and another in the race, one in Germany, and yet another in Hungary.

There was an upturn in Canada, where he banged in third fastest time in qualifying, but the decision to run with only one fuel stop immediately dropped him down the race order. He also snagged his front wing on the back of David Coulthard's McLaren, harming his SF-1's handling, and was given a ten second stop-and-go penalty for passing Mika Salo's Tyrrell under a yellow flag. In the end, gearbox failure rendered it all academic.

Within the team the performance of Ford's ageing V10 was now a source of considerable concern. It was the last power unit in Formula One still to use chain-drive for its camshafts, and besides lacking competitive horsepower it was also woefully unreliable.

Magnussen headed Barrichello for a while in heavy rain in Belgium, where the Brazilian spun into retirement on the ninth lap, and while he actually got to the finish in Italy he was way off the pace in an eventual 13th place on a track where the car's acknowledged aerodynamic qualities should have helped.

It was not until the Austrian GP, on the new A1 Ring, that the team picked up again, partly thanks to the suitability of Bridgestone's tyres to the track. Barrichello qualified fifth and ran second to leader Jarno Trulli's Bridgestone-shod Prost for the first 24 laps, until champion-elect Jacques Villeneuve overtook him. After his final pit stop he was challenging Michael Schumacher for seventh place as he moved back up the field, when his engine broke yet again.

He qualified ninth at the Nürburgring, home of the Grand Prix of Luxembourg, and took advantage of a first-corner accident which saw Ralf Schumacher take off brother Michael, and had climbed up to third place by the 43rd lap when David Coulthard's McLaren broke its Mercedes engine. Just as Mika Häkkinen's car did likewise a lap later, and Barrichello was poised to take second place behind Villeneuve, hydraulic failure denied them another potential dream result.

There were only two races left. In Japan Barrichello spun off while pushing hard after Damon Hill's Arrows. Then in Jerez, for the Grand Prix of Europe (where, unusually, Magnussen narrowly outqualified him), another gearbox failure intervened.

The first year with Stewart, then, was a mixture mainly of bad with a small smattering of good. It was, as Jackie Stewart said, a case of climbing the learning curve. Overall, Barrichello had finished 14th in the World Championship for Drivers, on the strength of his six points scored in Monaco, but that became 13th when the FIA disqualified Schumacher after his controversial collision with Villeneuve in Jerez as they fought for the title. Stewart-Ford was ninth out of the ten teams which scored points in the Constructors' title chase.

Barrichello had been happy to open the door when Paul and Jackie Stewart came knocking, and theirs was a solid relationship which was really cemented by that extraordinary performance in Monte Carlo. The former champion and his son worked so hard to give him the right car with which to express his talents, and Barrichello felt relaxed in a situation where Paul and Jackie so obviously had the same sort of relationship as he had with his own father.

Gary Anderson was confident that Barrichello had done exactly the right thing. 'The move to Stewart for 1997 was exactly what he needed, again a young team relying on him and working closely with him. This is the environment he thrives in, and also a team-owner like Jackie that does know what he is talking about was a great asset to allow Rubens to grow in confidence again. He definitely didn't have that at Jordan.'

While the Stewarts set about correcting the shortcomings for 1998, Ford also had a lot of soul-searching to do. Attitudes had to be changed, particularly at Cosworth Engineering where critics were suggesting it was time for Cosworth to do rather more of what Ford wanted and rather less of what it wanted, for Cosworth had a reputation then of being somewhat complacent and arrogant.

Yet though everybody began looking forward with tremendous enthusiasm to 1998, it would prove to be just another season that would flatter only to deceive with cruel monotony.

Stewart and Ford completely revised their gameplans for the new season. For a start, there were new regulations, which mandated cars with narrower track and grooved tyres in an attempt to reduce grip and cornering speeds, and to increase lap times in the interest of safety. Every designer was obliged to pursue fresh avenues of research, and this undoubtedly benefited those who were sufficiently wealthy and organised to test interim cars partway through 1997. Stewart Grand Prix had been too busy working to hone the SF-1 to have any chance of conducting such empirical experiments.

This would have one effect; another was the withdrawal of Goodyear. This meant that Bridgestone now began to supply the whole field, and now that it was working with more successful teams who had better chances of winning, Stewart also lost the advantage of near exclusivity it had enjoyed with the Japanese manufacturer in 1997. Due to the monopoly situation, Bridgestone now also had little incentive to develop new compounds and constructions, something else that had helped Stewart the previous year.

The good news was that the points from Monaco had won the team its FOCA membership as it became a signatory to the new Concorde Agreement for 1998. This saved a considerable amount of money on travelling, which could now be diverted into areas of development on the car. Behind the scenes, designer Alan Jenkins and technical director Egbahl Hamidy had totally refined the SF-1 to create the SF-2, which the Stewarts hoped would help to make them a top six team that could consistently qualify in the top ten and finish regularly in the points. At the same time, Cosworth created a completely new V10 engine that featured belt-driven camshafts for the first time and was better suited to the shape of a modern Formula One car. This helped Jenkins and Hamidy to optimise the technical package better. Ford also put greater technical resource at the team's disposal, and this was particularly important in one key area. The SF-2 would use a complex but advanced carbon fibre gearbox casing in place of the conventional cast aluminium unit favoured by most other teams.

The problems, however, started early. Where the team had had all of 1996 to prepare for its entry in 1997, now it was part of the racing scene there were delays in completing the SF-2s, and they were still being worked on frantically in the paddock in Melbourne at the first race. The mechanics worked late into the night getting Barrichello and Magnussen cars that they could drive. It was not the way to go racing, as the Stewarts knew only too well, and it set the tone for the bitterly disappointing season that was to follow.

Barrichello qualified 14th but never even got off the line at the start as his gearbox failed. It was an ignominious start, compounded when Magnussen crashed while fighting with Ralf Schumacher on the second lap. In Brazil Barrichello suffered another transmission failure as Magnussen finished tenth, and in Argentina their respective positions and retirements were reversed.

By Imola, the first European race of the year, it was clear that there were serious tensions between Stewart and Ford. All the time Cosworth's V10 had been emulating a grenade in 1997, the Stewarts had maintained a diplomatic silence, never voicing a word of criticism of their engine supplier. But now many Ford and Cosworth representatives were openly critical of the Stewarts' side of the operation, and in particular the gearbox. They accused them of taking on an engineering project that was far too complex for a small team. Privately, the drivers doubtless agreed. The animosity was compounded by suggestions that Ford was thinking of switching to the Jaguar brand. While the Stewart-Ford tag had a ring to it, sceptics doubted that Jaguar would want anything but Jaguar in the title. Already there were suggestions that Ford would soon buy the Stewarts out of the team they had created. More ominously, there were also rumours that a Ford representative had approached Benetton to see if it was interested in rekindling its past relationship which had resulted in a world title in 1994.

All of this was preying on Barrichello's mind that weekend, which turned out to be a complete disaster when Magnussen crashed into the back of his car at the start. For the second time that year Barrichello didn't get past the opening lap, while Magnussen's gearbox chewed itself up within eight laps.

By now Barrichello was seriously beginning to wonder what he was doing. He had a great relationship with the team, but like

Jordan in 1995 and 1996, he was no longer sure where it was going. Fortunately the Spanish Grand Prix in Barcelona brought a much-needed fillip when he qualified ninth, made a superb start, and kept Williams's World Champion Jacques Villeneuve and Sauber's Johnny Herbert behind him all the way to an honourable fifth place.

Hopes were high as Monaco was the next race on the calendar, bearing in mind that the big upturn had come there the previous year, but only disappointment awaited the team. Both Barrichello and Magnussen retired with broken suspension without doing anything impressive.

If Spain seemed to have been a false dawn, the sky lightened in Canada as Barrichello led Magnussen home in fifth and sixth places, after both of them avoided getting involved in not one but two first corner shunts. And had he not begun to suffer brake fade on a circuit that places massive demands on a car's stopping power, Barrichello was confident he could have mounted a challenge against former teammate Eddie Irvine's Ferrari for the final podium place.

Stewart then moved back to Europe for the French Grand Prix, where Dutchman Jos Verstappen replaced Magnussen. Now there was a feeling that things were getting on to a more even keel, but unbeknown to anyone Stewart Grand Prix had already scored its final points of the year.

Barrichello led Verstappen home, in 10th and 12th places, in France, and for the second year running both cars dropped out of their home grand prix at Silverstone with engine failures. In Austria the weather generated confusion in qualifying but Barrichello once again judged the situation well to take fifth place on the grid. He was fighting with Michael Schumacher's Ferrari over fourth place when a brake problem sent him to the pits after only nine laps.

The remainder of the year was a blur of poor performance, gearbox failures, and disillusionment. At Hockenheim and Hungaroring the gearbox failed; at Spa he suffered another start-line collision and his third early retirement of the season; Monza brought a lowly tenth place finish, Nürburgring 11th; at Suzuka the differential ingested itself after 26 laps.

In the final analysis, Rubens Barrichello finished 12th in the drivers' championship with four points; Stewart Ford managed eighth, one place better than 1997, with five points. It was nowhere good enough.

Now the political infighting reached fever pitch as the rumours about Ford's future flew and criticism mounted over the Stewart SF-2's carbon gearbox. Whatever had made Stewart think it could overcome the sort of problems that had made Ferrari shelve its own similar design? Everyone had expected the second season would be tougher than the first, but nobody had expected it to be so gruelling. The lateness in completing the SF-2 and its belt-driven version of Ford's Zetec-R V10 had denied the team the testing mileage it needed before the season began, and it had never really recovered the lost momentum.

While all this was going on, Barrichello had been considering his options, and knew that both Frank Williams and BAR were interested in his services. 1998 was enough to make any driver at least ponder what else was available, but once Barrichello learned that Williams was not interested in paying to buy out the remainder of his Stewart contract, he stopped looking at what at the time seemed greener grass, and settled down again into his habitual role of morale booster. That was a huge relief for a team that had been built around a driver that everyone within it still rated very highly. The outside world might be in danger of writing off Rubens Barrichello, but at Stewart they knew a good thing when they saw it.

Taking stock, he had seen off both teammates, Magnussen and Verstappen. The Dane had shown great potential, racing Barrichello hard on his debut for McLaren at TI Aida in 1995, but the Brazilian had the upper hand virtually throughout their 18 months together at Stewart. Some theorised that Magnussen missed the counsel of his brother, who had acted as his interpreter during his highly successful karting and Formula Three days; others that his enforced seasons of ITC racing with Mercedes-Benz, which followed his great year of Formula Three with Paul Stewart Racing in 1994, had taught him bad ways which he could not resolve. Whatever, Barrichello's reputation as top dog remained intact, and Jos Verstappen never came close to challenging it in his short stay.

Looking back, Barrichello thought that the problems of the year had more to do with the car than the engine. 'In 1997 the performance of the car was actually very good, and the aerodynamics were very good. But they took a small step with performance and a bigger one with reliability this year. The SF-2 had tremendous understeer on the grooved tyres, and it just wasn't up to the competition at all. The only track it liked was Barcelona. We discovered eventually that the real problem was that the chassis flexed.'

Jackie Stewart pulled no punches as he summarised the season. 'I think it's fair to say that we failed to be as competitive as I think we could have been in the latter part of year two, but the lessons of 1998 have been heeded. What has to be remembered is that we are still only in our third year of competition and we have achieved an awful lot in that short space of time. We have probably achieved more than any other modern Formula One team particularly when you consider we started from scratch.'

But the Nürburgring typified the frustration of the year, as Barrichello drove balls out just to finish 11th in the Grand Prix of Europe. It was a reminder of what people so often overlook about Formula One: even the drivers of the cars that finish way back are driving to their maximum. But somehow Barrichello was able to draw some satisfaction from the sheer consistency of his lap times, as he explained: 'Nobody looked at my sequence of times from that race, but I qualified at 1m 21.2s and raced all through at 1m 22.9, 22.8, 22.9. That's not bad. When I do that, I feel that I have so much to give to a team. I feel that my time has to come.

That I'm gonna get my chance. In 1994 with Jordan I had a good car but it didn't have a really strong engine. But I was there; I finished on the podium, I had a pole position, but people just forget that. There's a lot of that in F1. Why is it that drivers who are supposed to be very good never deliver? Because they didn't get a good car. So they relax. They were well paid, but they relaxed ...'

He was determined he would not fall into that trap, but admitted that keeping up his motivation after five or six bad races stretched him to the limit. 'I kept motivated because we were just in front, or just behind, the Prost. And you have to think of that, otherwise you lose it. I have to say that in the middle of that race at the Nürburgring, I asked myself, "Why are you doing this?" And all of a sudden the answer came: "I do this because I love it, and I'm going to do well even if I'm only gonna finish 11th." If you compare my race with Jos's ... I did very well. The car was very bad, and I wasn't gonna get any points, but I was just racing and I drove that one flat-out. From that point of view it was one of my best.

'I just always keep the thought that my chance will come. A better car will come. That keeps me motivated. But, sure, there are times when it's difficult to maintain that upbeat belief. But you just have to ...'

Early in November that year some key changes occurred at Ford that would have telling consequences. Neil Ressler, Vice President and Chief Technical Officer of Research and Vehicle Technology for Ford, was appointed Chairman of Cosworth Racing. Dick Scammell MBE, who had been acting as interim managing director, would work with him to oversee the transition of Cosworth Racing into its new position as a fully-owned Ford subsidiary.

Almost overnight it was as if people such as Formula One project leader Nick Hayes had been liberated. Now he was free from Ford's corporate fetters he could pursue his own avenues of development. Fortunately, he had been doing this for much of

At Imola in May 1990, Barrichello leads the GM Opel Lotus field for Draco Racing.

Victory at Silverstone in July 1990 was a sweet moment as the Brazilian's European career blossomed. He would come to regard the Northamptonshire circuit with great affection as the scene of some of his most memorable drives.

Left: *As Barrichello prepares to make his British Formula Three debut at Silverstone in March 1991, he receives advice from the former incumbent of West Surrey Racing's number one Ralt, world champion-to-be Mika Häkkinen.*

Below left: *Heading for second place at Thruxton in May 1991, with title challenger David Coulthard right in his wheeltracks. He'd started from pole but would need to set fastest lap to make up for a poor start which cost him victory.*

Right: *Though Barrichello maintained his career momentum by winning the 1991 British Formula Three championship, not every day was a happy one!*

Below: *Race engineer Roberto Trevisan was hugely impressed when Barrichello took his Il Baronne Ramparte F3000 Reynard to third place on his first acquaintance with the tricky street circuit at Pau in 1992.*

Above left: *A brace of Rubens Barrichellos: Rubinho with the man who plays such a great part in his life, father Rubens Snr. They even share the same birthday.*

Left: *Barrichello quickly gelled with the Jordan team in 1993, earning the respect of team manager John Walton (left) and designer Gary Anderson (right).*

Above: *In only his third Grand Prix, Barrichello drove like a star in the fickle conditions at Donington Park in 1993, where he should have joined his hero Ayrton Senna on the podium.*

Right: *Barrichello enjoyed an uneasy relationship with Jordan teammate Eddie Irvine, who burst on the scene at Suzuka in 1993.*

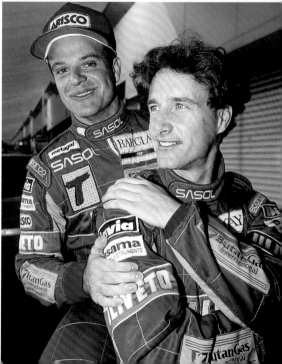

Above left: *Barrichello is a friend to many people in the world, not just in the paddocks of Formula One.*

Above right: *That fateful weekend at Imola in 1994, a carefree Barrichello enjoyed a charity football game in Forli on the Thursday night.*

The sequence of Barrichello's accident at Imola is chilling. As the Jordan Hart strikes the safety fence the magnitude of the impact and his good fortune in surviving it are evident. Once the car came to rest, Professor Sid Watkins and his medical crew were at the scene literally within seconds.

Ayrton Senna was one of the first people Barrichello saw in the medical centre as he recovered. Here the two friends discuss the accident. Neither could possibly know it would be their last conversation.

Everywhere that Barrichello went after Imola in 1994, there were poignant reminders of Ayrton Senna.

The 1994 season was not all sadness: Spa in August brought Barrichello the first pole position of his career after intelligent assessment of changing weather conditions.

1995 was becoming something of a disaster, until Barrichello turned a metaphorical corner by taking an excellent second place finish – his best to that point – in the Canadian Grand Prix.

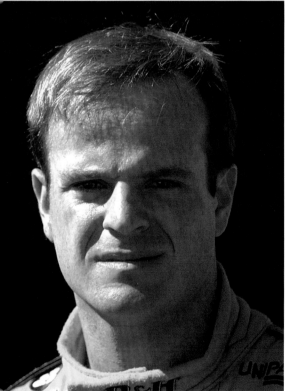

Above: *The 1996 season started well, as Barrichello found himself with a car strong enough to fight with Michael Schumacher's Ferrari in the rain in Interlagos.*

Left: *Before long, however, things began to get on top of the emotional Brazilian, whose final year with Jordan would not be a happy one.*

Above right: *Barrichello pulls off a daring late overtaking move on Heinz-Harald Frentzen in the 1996 Canadian GP, pushing the Jordan round the outside of the German's Sauber C15.*

Right: *In practice at Monza in 1996, an increasingly frustrated Barrichello ponders his lot after his Jordan ground to a halt out on the circuit.*

Above left: *At Stewart, Barrichello found all the camaraderie that had gone missing at Jordan, working with Jackie and Paul Stewart and teammate Jan Magnussen.*

Left: *Brazilians flocked to Monte Carlo in 1997 in expectation of seeing their hero perform, but in poor weather conditions he would exceed even their wildest dreams.*

Above: *After moving swiftly into contention with the leading bunch, Barrichello – seen here pushing his Stewart-Ford through Ste Devote – worked through to a glorious second place behind Schumacher.*

Right: *Having parked alongside the victorious Schumacher in front of the Royal Box, an incredulous Barrichello raises his arms aloft in salute to his approaching Stewart teammates.*

Barrichello was particularly pleased in 1999 to be working again with his old friend, designer and race engineer Gary Anderson.

Leading in Brazil, 1999: the Stewart SF-3 was good enough to allow Barrichello to lead for many laps, albeit on a different fuel strategy to its principal rivals.

Good or bad, fair or foul, Rubens Barrichello Snr has always been there to share his son's highs and lows.

One of the 1999 season's several high points was a storming drive to fourth place in the Italian Grand Prix at Monza.

At the Italian track, however, the news was out that Barrichello, seen walking past a Ferrari truck, would be driving for the Prancing Horse in 2000.

Stewart's greatest day as a constructor came at the Nürburgring when Johnny Herbert won the 1999 European Grand Prix. Here on the podium with Stewart, runner-up Jarno Trulli, and Herbert, Barrichello betrays none of the disappointment he must have been feeling after being upstaged by his teammate.

Chapter 7

ATTENTION SEEKING:
STEWART, 1999

I n February 1999 Rubens Barrichello arranged the sort of event you rarely see these days in Formula One. He invited a bunch of journalists to go tenpin bowling in Bayswater, prior to lunch at Monza restaurant in Knightsbridge.

The beginning of any season, before the first race redefines reality, is always a great time in Formula One. No matter who and what dominated the previous season's racing, fresh hope always blossoms in every camp together with the belief that fortunes can, and will, be improved. Everybody has analysed where they went wrong and set about making suitable amendments, and the inevitable hyperbole has its roots in their justifiable pride in the effort they have expended. Much of the time people who work so close to the grindstone have little time to appreciate that even their successful rivals are doing precisely the same thing, and often the status quo continues unchanged. But every so often a team really does make a big step forward and the result is a significant improvement in form.

Stewart Ford was such a team in 1999.

Before leaving the team after disagreements, Alan Jenkins penned a beautiful little race car, the SF-3, which was light, sleek, and aerodynamic. He had worked his way through every aspect of the unloved SF-2, making it better. Out went the troublesome carbon fibre gearbox casing, and in its place came a more conventional magnesium unit whose performance was easier to predict. Jenkins also paid serious attention to enhancing the torsional rigidity of the chassis, after the SF-2's unfortunate flexure. There was no shortage of ribald jokes within the team describing the SF-3's super-stiff chassis as 'the Viagra of F1!'

The most significant part of the car was hidden away behind the cockpit, however, and would always be covered up through the season whenever the engine cover was removed. This was Hayes's contribution, a little jewel of an engine called the Ford Cosworth CR-1 V10. It was short and super-light, which helped Jenkins to achieve optimal weight distribution and led to an improvement of the whole car's centre of gravity, which in turn led to knock-on improvements. In conjunction with re-optimised spring/damper and steering assemblies, the result was a car much better suited to the new front tyres which had to have four grooves for 1999, than the SF-2 had been to the triples grooves of 1998.

To demonstrate just how much weight had been saved in the engine, Hayes had an aluminium billet machined up like a silver handbag, and delighted in inviting journalists to lift it and try to guess how much had been saved. When the little white car with its Racing Stewart tartan stripes was unveiled at the *Autosport* Show in Birmingham in January, you could taste the optimism of a team that knew it had finally got things right.

'We have done everything in our power to be as well prepared for the 1999 season as we possibly can be,' Jackie Stewart said. 'The fact that the SF-3 turned a wheel as early as December 23rd last year is testament to that. The car we ran for that shakedown was completely new – a new chassis and a brand new engine. We are further ahead with the development of SF-3 than we could possibly have forecast six months ago and I believe we are further advanced for the 1999 season than any of our competitors.

'We made a commitment that the team would not allow itself to get into the position we were in for the first race of the 1998 season in Melbourne, where we were ill-prepared. I said at the time that I will never let that happen again and I made a personal pledge to our team personnel who had worked hideous hours prior to that race that it wouldn't.'

Stewart expressed his confidence about the year ahead, and the belief that the team was on the threshold of delivering success on a regular basis. The feeling was that all the hard work for 1999 would prove fruitful, after the harsh lessons of 1998.

Stewart added something else, something that other team owners included without a second thought at their new car launches, but which was completely out of character for the former champion. 'With this car I believe that, if circumstances are favourable to us, we could win a race. We would need luck, but I believe we could do it in the right circumstances.'

This was why Barrichello was so relaxed, that February day in Bayswater. He had his close relationship with his father to provide a steadying influence, though recently his life had changed and he had matured after his marriage to Sylvana. The new lifestyle obviously suited him, and he let slip that one of his favourite things was arriving home to find her car already parked in the garage.

'I have a better relationship than ever with my father, but now I'm married and last year I didn't see him for four months. But that's my life now. I tell him now, "Come to Europe, come to races, watch and cheer for me. Don't worry about my contract." But I still go back and ask his advice at times.'

There was also the prospect of another young Brazilian in Formula One, helping to spread the burden of national expectation. This was Formula 3000 star Ricardo Zonta. 'I wish him all the best in F1, and that he doesn't go through some of the mistakes that I went through,' Barrichello said, with genuine concern. 'He's highly rated, and though I don't really know him, I do know that he's very quick. I hope he goes through a better time. I hope Geraldo, my old manager, can teach him from the mistakes I made.'

And he wasn't sitting on his thumbs waiting for his luck to turn. Instead, he was staying as upbeat as possible while simultaneously doing everything he could to make that luck himself. He was tougher, harder in some ways than in the past.

Without being arrogant he had fashioned a harder shell around himself as protection, but you only noticed it when he needed to push for what he believed he needed within the team. He was no pushover, but he was no monster, either. His placid character sat with him in the cockpit, where he exhibited a fluid smoothness with minimal sideways interruption to forward progress. It was significant, in the era of unforgiving, rock-hard grooved tyres, that he was more often than not one of the few drivers not to visit the gravel traps during a race weekend.

The bad luck had honed him, somehow, but he was as optimistic as ever. As things turned out, that game at Queensway Bowl encapsulated the season just gone, and the season to come. Like any race driver, Barrichello was already there when his guests arrived, fully warmed up and reeling off strikes with great panache. Psychology is everything. The wide smile was already working overtime.

'My grandfather was third in the world championship for boule,' he said, and it was difficult to know whether he was being serious, though easy to imagine the comment being true. Once the game began, however, and our opponents' team got off to a better start, Barrichello tried too hard and slipped into a frustrating bad patch. As one of his teammates, it was interesting to watch his reaction at first hand. Bowling is like race driving, or anything else that requires skill, precision, and a cool head. If you let yourself get angry or frustrated, and lose your real focus, the result is often that you do the thing badly that you so desperately want to do well. The harder you try, the less natural and more forced your approach, the worse you perform. But Rubinho realised this, calmed himself down, worked at it, and suddenly achieved a spare and backed it with a strike. He and his team were on the verge of victory when a local power cut brought the game to a premature and inconclusive halt. For some reason, elsewhere in the bowl, the inter-linked Daytona NASCAR racing games were still working. Predictably, nobody got close to the Brazilian on them as he reeled off triumph after triumph.

He remained his usual relaxed and affable self all through an enjoyable lunch at Monza, where the ambience and décor reflect a love of motor racing. 'Stewart was like my first year in Formula One, but with four years' experience,' he said. 'That's why I feel I'm still on my way up. The speed is there, and the mind is there too. Last year it didn't matter to me what Jan or Jos did, I was just doing things my own way. This year it doesn't matter what Johnny Herbert does as my new teammate. He can help the whole situation because he is more experienced, and if he is doing a much better job, it doesn't matter. I will still do things my own way, and that's why I feel I have come out of the black clouds again.

'Okay, this is my third year here. People say drivers get slower as they get older, but they never do. They just lose motivation and application. That's why I feel so fired up this year. I haven't lost my motivation at all.'

If there was a cloud in his sky, it was that people still underrated him, regarded him as a once promising star who never quite delivered. But he had tested the new Stewart SF-3 already at that stage and he knew just how good it was going to be. He could bide his time, and then he would prove his critics wrong.

'All the people who have worked with me, if you interview them one-by-one – I think they know what I am capable of doing. Even Eddie Jordan. I think when I've done badly it's been written that way, but I don't feel it's necessarily been written up when I've done well. I don't think what I've done well has always been recognised.'

There was no rancour in his comments, he was just reiterating his feelings and his determination to have his day in the sun.

'If I was in a smaller team I might think, "Oh Hell, we had a bad year and now we're gonna have another one. But Jackie did not just tell me he was gonna do things, he *did* them. I saw his plans and I contributed to them, and everything is going in the right direction. We have four cars ready right now, that's fabulous. In Melbourne last year, half an hour through qualifying, my car was still up in the air, being finished. That was a good lesson for me. I told myself, "So now Rubens, you are the quickest driver in the world. What do you do? You've got ten minutes left to qualify the car. You drive because you love it, so qualify the car." And in five minutes I did what I might have taken an hour to do. It was a good lap.

'But now we are ready in advance. Now our car is different. I don't yet know how good compared to the opposition, but we are gonna beat our times from last year by one second or more even if the tyres are slower. The engine has a lot more power at the top end, and the straightline speeds are up. I really have to clap my hands for Ford. They have done a great job, and Cosworth have been at their maximum. I do think it's one of the best engines so far this year. There has been a reliability problem, but it's in hand. There's a different attitude there. We're pushing the revs hard, we're not holding back.'

It had been a little boost that Williams and BAR had been interested in him for 1999, but even though his contract ran until the end of the year and the Stewarts weren't about to let him go, he wasn't particularly inclined to move in any case once he saw the plans for the new year. 'I had to be open-minded for a better chance,' he said by way of explanation, 'but if the car is very good this year ...' he paused, giving his audience time to focus on what he was about to say, 'Stewart will win a grand prix soon.'

Compared with what had happened in 1998, it was a preposterous thing to say if you didn't already know what other people in the team, from the Stewarts to Nick Hayes to Herbert, privately felt about the SF-3. Clearly Barrichello was not making the remark merely for show, but because he really believed it. He was enjoying his life at Stewart – in Formula One – once again, much more than he had after three years at Jordan. 'Now I have my feet on the ground. At Jordan towards the end I felt that someone came with a knife at my back, and thought, "Jesus, how did that happen?" And for 1997 I promised myself that, though I was effectively downgrading going to Stewart, which was a new team, that was never gonna happen again. You would never see me unhappy on the track again. I was going to enjoy myself, I was going to start again, and help myself with the four years of experience I had.

'Now I feel a changed man. I'm happier than ever, quicker than ever. And my mind is working. It doesn't matter whether Jackie likes me or not, or if Johnny is doing this or that. I have to do my own work, have a very good relationship with my engineers, and mind my own business. My father has always told me, "Son, take time. You're not going to learn how to be 40 at 22. Learn the lessons by line." He was right.'

Stewart, of course, *did* like Barrichello. He liked him very much. And he rated him.

'Rubens is one of the most impressive young men currently out there,' the former champion said warmly. 'He is fast and he is smooth and he uses his head all the time. He doesn't make many mistakes and he takes little out of the car. He is fit and well liked within the team, to which he contributes a lot. He is one of the best drivers and he will show that this year, I have no doubt.'

Knowing that Stewart valued him was doing wonders for Barrichello's confidence. 'Watching on one corner at Jerez with Jackie recently was something else, because he can see things that are quite clear. He can see what makes a driver, he has good eyes. And whenever he talks of me, he is not talking bullshit. He rates me as one of the best drivers out there. And I hope that that's true. I really believe in myself, and I am just waiting for my car. I cannot have a situation where I'm waiting, but waiting seated. I must be on my toes, working my way through, and that is going to make it a lot better for me when I win.'

He'd had his psychological ups and downs during his six years in Formula One, but was now one of the more balanced characters. He could look at former rivals such as Mika Häkkinen, David Coulthard, or Damon Hill, and not feel jealous about the greater success they had enjoyed. Coulthard had won grands prix already, Hill was the 1996 world champion, and Häkkinen, his predecessor at West Surrey Racing in Formula Three, had been crowned the champion in 1998. 'I don't regret things, I cheer for them,' he said. 'They worked as hard as they could and they got their chance. That makes me feel that I will have *my* chance. I have worked hard and I will keep working hard, and I feel sure because of that that my time will come. That is very clear in my mind. I've paid my dues. I sometimes wonder what I've done to deserve some bad things, but a lot of people can say that and they are behind me, so let's just do the right things and keep moving ahead. I'm better; ask Gary [Anderson], he'll tell you!'

That was the other factor that had made him so optimistic for the new season. With the departure of Jenkins, former Jordan technical director Gary Anderson had arrived at Stewart. There was always strong chemistry between the Brazilian and the big Irishman, and Barrichello was delighted. 'He's a workaholic, and I'm proud to say I was the first one to approach him for the Stewart job. He's made friends here quickly, and he's fantastic. He brings with him so much knowledge.'

'1999 was a good year and we got some good results,' Anderson recalled. 'We should have been even better but early season engine reliability cost us dearly.'

With only slightly better fortune, Barrichello might have won Stewart and himself their maiden victory in Melbourne, as the Stewart SF-3 quickly proved itself to be one of the most competitive cars on the grid.

Both drivers loved the new car, even though Herbert had suffered a nasty rear wing failure at maximum speed down the straight at Barcelona during testing. He had been lucky to walk away with a stiff neck and a bruised knee.

'The new car is much better than the old one in all respects,' Barrichello enthused. 'And the new engine has a lot more power than last year's, for sure, especially at the top end. The other impressive thing is the team itself. Last year we got to Melbourne well behind schedule, and I had my car running for only five minutes of qualifying. But before Melbourne this time I tested our fourth SF-3 chassis. Jackie said last year that he would never let the team get into such a situation again, and he has been absolutely true to his word. We have never been better prepared. That gives me great confidence.'

Anderson had settled in comfortably, and already it seemed as if he had been with the team since it started out on the F1 trail. 'It's nice to be where we are even if there's a lot of stuff we need to do,' he said. 'A hell of a lot has gone wrong for us, for sure, and we are confused by the damping right now, we're really not getting on top of that. It's our own system, but the concept initially was quite complex and it's been a bit of a pain. It's like anything, you've got to keep on. McLaren are obviously strong, and they're clever enough to get the car where they want it. Ferrari aren't going to be down for ever, and you'll need to be quite strong to keep up with them. But we have our own plan in place and there's quite a lot of development stuff in the pipeline.'

Now the performance in Melbourne had confirmed the promise the car had otherwise shown in testing, but it was all going up in flames. The trouble was, the SF-3 was literally the hottest car on the grid, both Barrichello's (fourth fastest) and Herbert's (11th) igniting themselves as they sat waiting for the red lights to go out. The cruel stroke of fortune came as small oil leaks ignited on the hot exhausts as the cars idled just before the off. Had they got going immediately, airflow would probably have killed the flames, but they sat still for just a little too long.

'I just couldn't believe it,' Jackie Stewart admitted. 'I just thought, "Aw, God!" It was a situation we'd never experienced in testing.'

When the original start was aborted so that the two fiery Stewarts could be wheeled away, Barrichello, as the faster qualifier, had claim to the spare car and started from the pit lane. From there he stormed through the field, catching the leading group as an accident involving Jacques Villeneuve's BAR brought out the safety car, but he was unlucky on the restart as Mika

Häkkinen's McLaren surged as Barrichello hovered alongside, momentarily placing the Stewart ahead, against the regulations, before they crossed the start/finish line. That resulted in the stewards levying a ten second stop-and-go penalty. After serving that he came home fifth, behind his victorious former teammate Eddie Irvine in the Ferrari, Heinz-Harald Frentzen's Jordan, Ralf Schumacher's Williams, and Giancarlo Fisichella's Benetton. He was both frustrated and elated.

'I could have won, I could have won,' he yelled, and the words came tumbling out. 'For the first time I had a car that allowed me to race and to overtake. I know that if I had started from my proper fourth place I could have won. We had a car that could perform well, and we did that. I'm happy to finish fifth. But I'm just upset that it was a race I could have won. I tell you, it was one of the best races of my career. I was so upset, because I could have been on that podium.'

Jackie was philosophical. 'The reality is that the car's obviously quite good. We were disappointed the way things turned out, but to come away with fifth place ... thank you very much! We know now that we have a good package that is going to be good all season.'

There was a time in Brazil when things looked even rosier, as Barrichello thrilled his expectant compatriots by qualifying third – ahead of Michael Schumacher – and led the race for a while after Häkkinen's McLaren suffered transmission gremlins. A Brazilian driver in a Scottish-run car led the Brazilian Grand Prix for 23 glorious laps, and even though that owed a little to the reduction in weight because of the two-stop strategy they had adopted compared to other rivals' single stoppers, it was still very impressive and endorsed every upbeat comment the team had made in the build-up to the season.

When the bigger teams regained their momentum after their fuel stops, Barrichello inevitably slipped back, but he was still on course for a great podium finish when the engine broke because of a gudgeon pin problem on the 43rd of the 72 laps. Before the first race Cosworth had yet to do a test in which the CR-1 engine revved to 17,250 rpm, and had allowed the drivers only 16,500 in Melbourne. Now it had given them full revs, and they proved too much. It was disappointing, but overall the performance was a tremendous boost to everyone in the team after 1998, not least the delighted driver.

At Imola in May Barrichello finally got his just desserts, as his car proved fast and reliable on its way to third place, and the team's first podium finish since Monaco 1997. Only Schumacher and Coulthard were ahead after the 62 laps. as Barrichello raced with the full 17,250 rpm to take the final podium slot. For Stewart, it was almost as good as a win, given how competitive the car had been all afternoon.

Suspension failure took both cars out of the Monaco Grand Prix, when Barrichello was headed for fifth place, and though he finished eighth in Spain he lost the placing afterwards when his car failed the post-race ride height test after the wooden undercar plank had worked loose.

It was, nevertheless, already a much better season than 1998, and the SF-3 was living up to expectations. The improvement was also reflected in qualifying, when at Monaco the team recovered from an upset in set-up caused by a change in weather conditions to put Barrichello seventh and Herbert 14th on the grid.

The team was three seasons old when it headed to Canada in June and there came the announcement that, ahead of schedule, its mentor Ford Motor Company had bought the team from the Stewarts. This had little effect on the team's on-track performance, which again seemed promising as Barrichello qualified fifth and Herbert tenth. Unfortunately for Barrichello, for the second year running Jarno Trulli collided with Jean Alesi going into the first corner, the Italian also striking the Brazilian's Stewart. That forced Barrichello into the pits for repairs, and he retired after 14 laps as the suspension had been pushed out of alignment. Herbert, however, drove strongly in a car whose marginal fuel capacity was particularly disadvantageous on a circuit where fuel consumption is always high, to take fifth place and his first points of the season.

Like Spa in 1994 or Austria the previous year, Magny-Cours faced changeable weather for qualifying, and yet again it was Barrichello who rose to the occasion to grab the only pole position Stewart Ford would achieve. At the start of the race he took the lead for the first five laps until having to yield to David Coulthard, but the Scot's McLaren rolled to a halt on the tenth lap with a faulty alternator, handing the advantage back to the Stewart. Just before Barrichello refuelled for the first time on the 22nd lap the rain returned with a vengeance, and though he kept his lead as everyone stopped at the same time, deployment of the safety car for ten laps when the rain reached its height (between laps 25 and 35) prevented him getting too far ahead.

When the racing resumed one danger receded as Jean Alesi spun out of second place, but on lap 38 Barrichello had to stand his ground as Mika Häkkinen tried an outbraking move at the Adelaide hairpin which resulted in the Finn spinning. Now the threat to Barrichello came from Michael Schumacher, who duly went ahead on lap 44. By lap 50 the German was 8.7s ahead, but a lap later Barrichello was right back with him. The Ferrari had developed a gearshift problem, and on lap 54 Schumacher dived into the pits for a new steering wheel in a bid to resolve an electronic glitch. Yet again Barrichello went back into the lead, but now his job was getting harder. His rear Bridgestones were going off, promoting oversteer and locking rear brakes. 'It was quite difficult to drive and I was having to concentrate hard,' he reported, 'but even so I was losing no time to the McLarens, Ferraris, and Jordans.' On lap 65 he lost the lead for the last time as he and the recovered Häkkinen refuelled, but unbeknown to either team Jordan's crew had given Heinz-Harald Frentzen a heavy fuel load on his first stop as they gambled on the track remaining wet, and he was just able to make the finish in the lead without having to refuel again. Häkkinen got out of the pits before Barrichello, so the Brazilian's great drive netted only third place instead of a possible second. But he was nevertheless delighted. 'This shows again what a strong team we are and what a great car we have,' he said. 'With just a little better fortune this was another race we could have won.'

Cruelly, after this performance, Silverstone yet again saw both Stewarts failing to score points, as the SF-3s were curiously off the pace. Barrichello finished only eighth and Herbert 12th.

Things picked up again in Austria, as Barrichello and Herbert qualified fifth and sixth, the Briton now beginning to push his teammate hard as, like Brundle in 1996 at Jordan, he finally felt fully confident in his car's set-up. Barrichello pushed hard after leader David Coulthard, both of them benefiting on the opening lap when the Scot inadvertently nudged teammate Häkkinen into a spin at the hairpin, but after his fuel stop on lap 38 the Brazilian had dropped down to fourth, behind Eddie Irvine, Coulthard, and Häkkinen; then his engine blew up on the 56th lap. It says much about the progress Cosworth had made that this was now a rarity, but for once Barrichello seemed tetchy as he said: 'The car felt good and my pace was consistent. But we have lost points too often this year when we have been well placed.' Herbert was delayed by a first-lap pit stop for a new rear wing after Mika Salo – standing in for Schumacher at Ferrari after the German broke his leg in a crash at Silverstone – ran into the back of him. After that the Briton set the race's second fastest lap while recovering to 14th place.

Hockenheim was equally disappointing, Barrichello falling out with hydraulic failure after seven laps, Herbert with a broken gearbox after 41. Hungary yielded Barrichello fifth place from eighth on the grid, and then the gremlins struck again at Spa where Barrichello finished only tenth. Monza, however, gave him another chance to shine. He qualified seventh, well clear of his troubled teammate, and set the third fastest lap while taking on and beating Coulthard's McLaren Mercedes and Mika Salo's Ferrari in straight fights early in the race. Salo got past again during the refuelling stops, but fourth place was a satisfying performance on such a fast track.

All season, Barrichello's speed made it seem a formality that, if Jackie Stewart's pre-season prediction of victory were to come true, it would be the Brazilian who scored it. But some brilliant judgement of unfavourable conditions, allied to a great driving performance, saw Herbert snatch the result in an extraordinary Grand Prix of Europe at the Nürburgring in September.

The Stewarts started only 14th and 15th on the grid after undistinguished qualifying performances, Herbert ahead, then ran 11th and 12th, in a reversal of that order, for the first nine laps. After 21 laps, however, as the skies darkened, they were fifth and seventh. Early leader Frentzen quit with electrical problems after 32 laps, then David Coulthard crashed his McLaren. Eddie Irvine and Mika Häkkinen were delayed respectively by a bungled tyre stop and a stop for the wrong choice of tyres. After Herbert's perfectly judged pit stop on lap 35, where he took a major gamble by changing to wet tyres, he found himself running ahead of Barrichello as the conditions worsened, and with Jarno Trulli's Prost between them and only Ralf Schumacher and Giancarlo Fisichella ahead. He then switched back to dry tyres on lap 47. Fisichella crashed his Benetton on lap 49, just after Schumacher's stop had handed him the lead, and then a lap later Schumacher crept to the pits with a punctured rear tyre. Suddenly, at the end of lap 50 and with only 16 to go, the Stewarts were running first and third, and Trulli had his hands far too full of the challenging Barrichello to worry about trying to catch Herbert. In the end the Briton ran home a surprise but worthy winner, the manner of his achievement endorsing Stewart's pre-season suggestion that, with luck and the right circumstances, the car could win. Effectively, Herbert's third Grand Prix victory was Jackie Stewart's 28th, and it would be his only one as a constructor. Trulli hung on to second, almost 23 seconds in arrears, with Barrichello only two-tenths further back.

By any standard it was a remarkable afternoon. On the podium, Herbert and Stewart were all smiles, and so, too, was Barrichello. It had to hurt, seeing the team he had helped to build win its first race with another driver at the wheel, especially after all his own near misses that year. Privately, he had to acknowledge that Herbert had driven every bit as well as he had in the race, but had used superior strategy with his gamble on tyres and his reading of the weather. Yet he kept his dignity and his smile demonstrated his genuine pleasure for his teammate, with whom he shared such a strong relationship.

'Rubens is a genuine guy,' Herbert said. 'A brilliant bloke. Fair and sporting. We had a lot of fun together, and I think we respected one another all season. You always know where you are with him. There is never any side to him, or any suggestion that he is trying to hide something from you.'

Barrichello might have said similar things about Herbert. 'I don't know Johnny very well, just from drivers' briefings, but the only thing I wish is that we keep our characters. We must beat each other at the track, but we must have our fun outside,' he said at the beginning of the year. 'Jan and I had fun together, and Johnny is a funny guy, the mechanics love his jokes.'

Now he showed his big heart by being one of the first to congratulate him. 'Johnny deserved to win,' he said. 'I know how hard it is to win races, and that he has had many hard times, and I am glad for him. It was very hard to make the decision when to stop and what tyres to run. That was the guess! Johnny guessed it right and I guessed it wrong! The team called me and asked, "Which do you want to go for, wets or dries?" First I said I wanted to go for wets, because the conditions were already marginal. But when I looked in front of me, what I saw was a clear sky, not the cloud that Johnny saw, so I thought the rain would go away faster than it did. And with the harder set of tyres that I had I was losing as much as five seconds per lap.'

Over the balance of the season, Herbert maintained the upper hand. At the inaugural Malaysian Grand Prix in Sepang he qualified fifth, one place ahead, and finished fourth, again one place ahead. But where Barrichello chose a conventional two-stop refuelling strategy Herbert opted for one and slugged it out with eventual third place man Mika Häkkinen before his worn rear tyres obliged him to concede the place to the McLaren. At one stage it seemed the two Stewarts might even be elevated to second and third positions when the two winning Ferraris were initially excluded for alleged bodywork infringements, but later the red cars were reinstated.

The Stewarts were not quite as quick in the final race, the Japanese Grand Prix at Suzuka, but once again Herbert outqualified Barrichello, eighth to 13th. In the race they finished seventh and eighth, Johnny ahead, but he could have been sixth but for a fumbled pit stop when his new tyres weren't ready.

And so ended the era of Stewart Ford, with Barrichello seventh overall with 21 points and Herbert eighth with 15, and the team an excellent fourth in the constructors' title chase with 36.

It had been a happy team, and the two drivers got on well. To begin with Barrichello had the upper hand on Herbert, who took time to acclimatise to the SF-3 and initially enjoyed poorer reliability and results before coming good at the end.

It had been known from July that Stewart Ford would metamorphose into Jaguar for 2000, and that Herbert would stay. And perhaps it was a private source of satisfaction to Barrichello that the Briton's new partner would be...Eddie Irvine. The Ulsterman was leaving Ferrari after four seasons, his last the most successful as he fought for the world championship with Häkkinen in Schumacher's enforced absence. But even more satisfying to Barrichello was the fact that he was the man who would replace Irvine alongside the greatest driver of his generation. The news had broken in September that he would be a Ferrari driver in 2000.

'Rubens has done a fantastic job for us all season, and in the two seasons prior to that, and I am confident that he will present a serious challenge to Michael Schumacher,' Jackie Stewart said.

Barrichello agreed fully with the Scot's latter point.

Chapter 8

Seeing red:
joining Ferrari in 2000

Rubens Barrichello had no illusions about the task he faced when the call came to join Scuderia Ferrari. It was Michael Schumacher's domain, and everyone there adored him. He was the best driver, and on top of that he was the man who had given the team back its self-respect. Thanks to the impetus he had given the team it had finally won the world championship for constructors in 1999, prising free the vice-like grip of McLaren and Mercedes-Benz, who in turn had superseded Williams Renault. It was the first time that Ferrari had won the constructors' prize since 1983. Now Schumacher was poised to become the Scuderia's first world champion since the South African Jody Scheckter way back in 1979. In all probability, only the broken leg he sustained at Silverstone in 1999 prevented it happening that year. He was the man everyone in Maranello would go to hell and back for.

Much of Ferrari's revival had been due to Schumacher's brilliance, and sporting director Jean Todt – while being careful to put a driver's role into its true perspective – was always unstinting in his praise. 'He is the world champion. He is a fantastic driver. Very professional, very motivated, very good spirit, a very hard worker. He is a point of reference for the team. Nevertheless, he is not a technical director or whatever, so he needs very much the support of the team. He is a driver, with all the fantastic things I just said about him.

'Humanly, he is a great guy. He's young, very mature, he loves driving, so for us it is fantastic to have him. But he deserves a good car and a good team. If he doesn't have that, no matter how good he is, he cannot work. He is very curious; he wants to know. He wants to understand but, again, he needs to be technically supported, which is normal.'

All of that could have been expected, given what Schumacher had helped Ferrari to achieve, but at times Todt had also been complimentary about Barrichello's old sparring partner, Eddie Irvine. 'Eddie is in a very difficult situation, because he is the number two,' Todt once said. 'At the start of each race he has exactly the same car as Michael. But in between races, priority is given to Michael for testing. Irvine is facing the best driver at the moment so it is very difficult for him, and he needs a very strong spirit. Of course we want to improve that situation, but it is very demanding of him. As a person he is very good in the team, and he has that strong spirit. He is a charming guy for the team, and a good driver. He is doing the best he can, and we are happy with him.'

In 1999 Irvine rose to the occasion brilliantly for Ferrari, winning all of his four grands prix victories in that season as he carried the torch with which Schumacher had burned his fingers in the British Grand Prix. But by Hockenheim and the German Grand Prix – which, ironically, Irvine won when Schumacher's stand-in Mika Salo moved over for him – Todt had already decided to drop the Ulsterman. Barrichello was under absolutely no illusion that he too might find himself between a rock and a hard place as he stepped into Irvine's seat. On the one hand, he would be expected to back Schumacher in everything and to run right in his wheeltracks; on the other, Schumacher held all the aces and, it was continually suggested, a contract that forbade his teammate from upstaging him in races. If he lagged too far behind the German he would be criticised, and if he didn't, if he really did find himself in a position to offer a genuine challenge to Schumacher, he would also probably be damned.

There were a lot of people who believed that driving the second Ferrari was a poisoned chalice, as long as Michael Schumacher was driving the first.

In some ways it was hard to fathom Barrichello's desire to go to Ferrari. Ayrton Senna had always envisaged ending his career there, but Barrichello regarded that as a poignant postscript, nothing more. He wasn't going to Ferrari for that reason, and he knew that Schumacher would be licking his lips like the Big Bad Wolf relishing the arrival of Little Red Riding Hood, but it was a sign of his own increasing maturity that he didn't feel threatened. He was adamant they would have equal status, that there was no 'no-overtaking' clause in his contract like there was in Irvine's. He understood why some people thought he was crazy to leave a team that so clearly loved him, and what the critics said about his occasionally vulnerable psyche, but he reminded people of one of his favourite beliefs: 'I've said it before: racing is like bowling, you try hard, get the spare, the strike. So much of this game is in the head, too. Chances like Ferrari don't come along very often. I'm confident enough in myself now to believe that I will do well there.'

As the doubting continued, he developed the theme at the first race of the 2000 season. 'I knew all the arguments,' he said in the paddock in Albert Park in Melbourne, his vivid red overalls still looking unfamiliar. 'I thought about it all very carefully, and came to the conclusion that nothing is ever for certain, in both life and in racing. Ferrari was the best possible team to join at that moment. It was on the rise and it had successfully challenged McLaren's superiority throughout 1999. In the end, I had no qualms about joining Michael. You have to believe in yourself 100 per cent in this game, and I believed in myself. If you want to win, you have to be prepared to put yourself up against the very best. I figured it was better to do that in the same equipment.'

At the beginning of the year Ferrari had promised that their two drivers would have equal status. 'Whichever of them is fastest will be the number one,' president Luca di Montezemolo told journalists at the launch of the new car. But even then people had their doubts. Few were taken in. Ferrari was Schumacher's team, and this was not the same situation as Ayrton Senna joining Alain Prost at McLaren back in 1988. The Ferrari team had been honed around Schumacher, he had helped to lead it back from the wilderness, and the only driver out there with equal talent was Häkkinen. And Schumacher would see that it stayed that way.

Barrichello, by contrast, was too much of a gentleman and too sensitive to survive in what was expected to be a tough environment, his critics suggested. He had simply picked too big a mountain to climb.

Schumacher gave absolutely no indication that the incident in which he had broken his leg at Silverstone the previous year had had the slightest effect on his psyche, and was a relentless force all through the new season as he sped to his third world drivers' championship and Ferrari's first since Scheckter 21 years earlier.

Barrichello opened his account well, qualifying fourth alongside Schumacher in Australia, less than a tenth of a second slower, and finishing second, 12 seconds behind with the fastest lap as the Scuderia got off to the best possible start.

At home in Brazil he again qualified fourth, and again he was alongside Schumacher whom he trailed by just over a tenth. Michael had damaged his intended race car with an off-course moment and used the spare car, while Rubens's final run was thwarted by red flags, but for which he might have taken second on the grid. Schumacher won the race, but after leading laps 21 and 22 during the first pit stops Barrichello was running fourth, behind Häkkinen, Schumacher, and Coulthard, when his hydraulics went awry on the 27th lap.

There was more disappointment at Imola on Ferrari's home ground, where Schumacher dominated yet again and won from Häkkinen and Coulthard in their McLarens, with Barrichello a distant fourth. For a time he had slowed up Coulthard, leading to suspicions that he was on a one-stop refuelling strategy in contrast to the others' two-stops, but it transpired that he was unhappy with the handling of the car and had a problem too with loose seat belts. Coulthard got by him during their second stops.

'I was never very confident in the set-up we had on the car,' Barrichello admitted. 'And I had a problem with the lower part of my belts and couldn't maintain a good pace as my legs were moving around too much.'

Shrugging off the Imola result, Barrichello lost little time stamping his authority in qualifying at Silverstone, for a British Grand Prix brought forward from its usual July date to April by politics. There he took his first pole position for Ferrari, in the sort of wet but drying qualifying conditions that he loves. 'I am particularly proud because in last week's test here I only had two days in the wet, so apart from the two laps I did yesterday, I had no experience with the car here in the dry.

'I went out quite early for my first run, which meant I was a little offset from the main group. I knew the car was good, I knew I could do a good job, so I had to go out for my last run with the main group and just pray not to have traffic.'

He was leading the race comfortably when he had more hydraulic problems. They manifested themselves in the worst possible way, as the Ferrari's gearshift baulked as he sped through the eye-of-the-needle esses at Becketts at 140mph on the 31st lap, which enabled the pursuing Coulthard to slingshot into the lead, but Barrichello retrieved it when the Scot refuelled two laps later. The Ferrari only lasted until lap 35, however. As he approached the pits for his own stop, the problem threw him into a spin in the final corner, and though he got going again he retired in the pits.

'I don't know what the problem was,' he said, ignoring those who suggested he had just made a mistake, 'but I was leading easily until it first arose. I'm very disappointed.'

Schumacher, who was beaten for the first time on that occasion by his new partner, finished third, unable to hold on to the silver Arrows of winner Coulthard and Häkkinen.

The German was back on pole in Spain, where Barrichello qualified third, half a second behind and kept off the front row by Häkkinen. In the race Schumacher led initially after blocking

Häkkinen, as Barrichello became embroiled in a fight with Ralf Schumacher's BMW Williams and Coulthard's McLaren. Then Schumacher inadvertently ran over Ferrari chief mechanic Nigel Stepney during his first pit stop, breaking the Briton's ankle, after lollipop man Federico Uguzzoni waved the champion back into battle prematurely. Subsequently a problem with his refuelling nozzle delayed Schumacher in his second stop, enabling Häkkinen through for the win. Schumacher then got into a scrap with Coulthard (about which the Scot, who had survived an air crash only days earlier that killed both pilots, had harsh words to say afterwards) before picking up a slow puncture. It was while the German was busy pushing his younger brother wide that Barrichello grabbed the BMW Williams driver's fourth position on lap 50, and this immediately became third as Schumacher Snr pitted to have his punctured tyre replaced. It made good television, and while Coulthard and Ralf were miffed with Michael, Rubens was left laughing all the way to the podium with Häkkinen and Coulthard after being bottled up behind his teammate's brother all through the race.

As it had the previous year when Johnny Herbert won for Stewart, the Grand Prix of Europe at the Nürburgring featured changeable weather, the race starting on a dry track but later being drenched by a rainstorm. Schumacher beat the McLarens after a virtuoso display, setting fastest lap as well, while once again Barrichello had to be content with fourth place, bottled up behind Coulthard for a long time, and troubled occasionally by baulky downshifts. 'I think the real problem was that I stayed out a lap too long on dry tyres,' he later admitted. 'I should have been on the podium today.'

Silverstone notwithstanding, it was by now clear that he was not posing as much of a threat to Schumacher's supremacy as he had hoped before the season started.

A string of podiums followed, however, with seconds at Monaco, where Schumacher started from pole but retired with damaged suspension, and in Canada, where Schumacher won;

and third in France, where once again the German was fastest in qualifying but dropped out with an engine failure.

It was Canada that showed the real state of affairs within Ferrari.

Schumacher led from pole position, his task made easier after Coulthard was subsequently penalised after stalling on the grid and restarting in contravention of Article 139 of the regulations. After overcoming fast-starter Jacques Villeneuve in the BAR Honda on the 25th lap, Barrichello moved up to shadow his team leader. Then it began to rain on lap 40, and that coincided with Schumacher experiencing brake problems which sent him off course on one occasion. Barrichello was clearly a lot faster now and closed right up. On lap 45 he elected to follow Schumacher in for rain tyres, knowing that this would delay him while he waited for his teammate to be serviced but believing that to do another lap on grooved tyres in the prevailing conditions would be asking for worse trouble.

'I lost so much time at the Nürburgring when I was late in for my stop, that I talked it over with the team on the radio and they gave me the option to come in with Michael. That's what I did.'

Once they were both running again he soon closed up on the troubled Schumacher, but team orders did not permit him to challenge. Since the closest challenger was Giancarlo Fisichella in the Benetton, some way back, Jean Todt left Schumacher out front and Barrichello followed him home again. They crossed the line 0.174s apart. Barrichello was doubtless cursing that on this occasion Coulthard had made an error on the grid that took his McLaren out of the equation, but he put a brave face on having to ride shotgun for Michael.

'I have no problem with backing off to protect him when I am asked to by the team,' he said, adding rather lamely, 'Besides, I had a problem with my clutch.' Cynical observers were not convinced.

Schumacher was certainly grateful for Barrichello's gentlemanly obedience of team dictates. 'He is a good man,' the former champion said, 'and one day I will pay him back.' He now led the title chase with 56 to Coulthard's 34 and Häkkinen's 32, partly thanks to Barrichello's help.

Austria saw Barrichello narrowly outqualify Schumacher, and he seemed to get more out of his Ferrari's set-up than Michael could on this occasion. Where Barrichello coaxed his time out of the car, Schumacher had to bully his. It was a bad weekend for the German, who became a victim of a first-corner incident after being nudged from behind by Ricardo Zonta in the BAR. Barrichello was able to settle down to chase the McLarens of Häkkinen and Coulthard home for third place and another podium. It was a good drive in the circumstances, after his car was damaged as a result of running over debris from the subsequent first-corner melee involving the Saubers, Jos Verstappen's Arrows, Jarno Trulli's Jordan, and Giancarlo Fisichella's Benetton, which happened in the wake of the Schumacher/Zonta incident. But he could not help feeling that his first victory could have been there for the taking.

It was the superfast Hockenheim circuit that provided the high point not just of Barrichello's season, but of his career to that point, for that was where he finally did win his first grand prix. As he will remember all his life, it was 30 July.

The previous day, however, things could scarcely have been worse, as he could only qualify 18th. There had been massive thunderstorms the previous day, and qualifying on the Saturday was held on a damp track amid intermittent rain. On Saturday morning Schumacher crashed his race car and took over the spare. When Rubens went out for qualifying his own race car stopped on the circuit with a fault in the electrics, and he ran back to take over Schumacher's damaged car, on which the mechanics were already working to alter it to suit Barrichello. The incident in the morning had damaged the rear wing and right-hand rear suspension, which had been fixed in case Schumacher needed it again, but the major problem was altering the pedals to suit a different driver. Schumacher liked left-foot braking; Barrichello still did not. The job dragged on, losing them what little dry running there was at the start of the session before the rain came back. As a result, where Michael had been able to lap in 1m 47.063s for second place on the grid, Barrichello managed only 1m 49.544s in greasy conditions and started from the ninth row. It did not seem to augur well.

What would be one of the most dramatic races of the year got off to a controversial start. From pole position Coulthard did to Schumacher what Schumacher habitually did to everyone else in the same situation, and swerved to the right across the road to block any challenge from the German. In retaliation Schumacher moved to the left as they sped to the first corner, and promptly collided with Giancarlo Fisichella's Benetton. Both retired on the spot.

In the excitement, it was Häkkinen who grabbed the lead from Coulthard and Jarno Trulli's Jordan. As the race moved past its midpoint the refuelling stops began, but then the safety car was deployed between laps 25 and 28 when a spectator began wandering along the side of the track by the first chicane. He was 47-year-old Robert Sehli, a Frenchman with a grudge against Mercedes-Benz after being made redundant on health grounds after working for them for 22 years, and who had already made a less successful attempt to disrupt the French Grand Prix. Eventually he was arrested and charged with trespass, but his presence had also upset the rhythm of the race and given a charging Barrichello a chance.

With 15 laps to go it began to rain on the pit straight section of the track, though the remaining two-thirds of the circuit remained dry. That made the decision whether to switch to wet-weather tyres or to stay on grooved slicks as tricky and as difficult as the driving conditions themselves. Complicating things further, the safety car was deployed again between laps 30 and 31 after Brazilian driver Pedro Diniz tripped up French charger Jean Alesi on the entrance to one of the chicanes.

The rain and the two safety car periods had upset several drivers' pit stop strategies. Coulthard, for example, dropped from second to fifth. BAR teammates Jacques Villeneuve and Ricardo Zonta took each other out, and Eddie Irvine also crashed. Through it all, Barrichello employed all his legendary throttle control and smoothness of touch to keep his Ferrari on the road and to push ever closer to the front. He had begun on a light fuel load, planning to make two pit stops where most of his rivals would make only one. Even allowing for that, some of his overtaking manoeuvres were breathtaking in their audacity and precision. It could have been Schumacher himself driving Ferrari number four as he laid the ghost of his Formula 3000 years. He was up from 18th on the grid to third place after 15 of the 45 laps, and took the lead on the 35th lap when Häkkinen finally pitted for rain tyres. But he seemed certain to lose it in his own subsequent pit stop.

Gradually it became clear that he would not be stopping, and as Häkkinen began to storm back to his eventual second place ahead of Coulthard, the Ferrari plugged on out front. Barrichello and technical director Ross Brawn had agreed to gamble on him staying out on his grooved slicks, and at last, in his 123rd grand prix, his courage would be rewarded. He beat Häkkinen, the back-to-back world champion, by 7.452 seconds.

On the podium, the tears flowed from an emotional man who was savouring the greatest day of his racing life. And there was probably not a soul in the paddock who begrudged him his overdue success. Later, the beaming smile was magnified. 'This is a team,' he said. 'We are a big family. Ross told me: "Mika is coming in," and I said, "I want to keep an eye on things, let's stay out for one lap more." After that lap he said, "Just keep on going, Rubens, because you're going to win if you keep up this pace."

'It was great, because the slicks were still doing really well on the straights and in the three chicanes. But with six or seven laps to go, I flat-spotted the left front at the third chicane, because it was spitting a little bit and I locked up. That was worrying, and I couldn't see the track very well because of the vibration. So I paid the price, but it worked out great.'

His maiden victory turned the championship chase into a four-man battle, with only 10 points separating the protagonists: Schumacher on 56, Häkkinen and Coulthard tying for second with 54, and now Barrichello on 46.

His last race victory had been in Formula Three at Silverstone on 6 October 1991, and he lost no time in making an emotional dedication. 'I'm dedicating this race to a guy on top there, Ayrton,' he said, looking skyward. 'It was since 1984 that he changed my life. I was really a racing driver from then onwards. I followed him very much. He listened to me quite a lot, and today is a good day to dedicate the race to him.

'After Ayrton left, a lot of people just put me into his place. A lot of people liked it, but a lot of people didn't, so I was in the middle of confusion. There is no one who just likes Rubens: either you love Rubens or you hate him. I just want to say thank you very much to the guys who stayed there for me, and principally my father.'

Over and over he savoured the feeling afterwards. 'I just feel great. On the last lap I heard the guys telling me I was going to win, but it's such a long lap here. Also, it's been such a long time (since my last victory) that I had almost lost the taste. And I can promise you that it was getting more and more tricky today, because the rain was falling in separate places. Yesterday was such a bad day that I was just thinking to myself that this one had to be mine. I told myself it could come good, so let's make it as simple as possible. But I still can't believe it.'

And his teammate was in congratulatory mood. 'I am very disappointed for what happened to me, but I am very happy for Rubens, whom I have to thank for saving my first place in the Drivers' Championship,' Schumacher said. 'His win was a very emotional moment for me.'

Schumacher started the Hungarian Grand Prix from pole position, but Häkkinen won the race from the German, with Coulthard third and Barrichello fourth, the Brazilian again disappointed not to match his teammate's race speed. Only quick pitwork got him ahead of Ralf Schumacher, behind whom he had long been trapped.

Schumacher was second again in Belgium, where Häkkinen sensationally overtook the German on the approach to Les Combes as they darted either side of a stunned (and lapped) Ricardo Zonta. Barrichello had another miserable outing, qualifying only tenth after struggling all through qualifying to find the right set-up. When he finally began to put a good lap together he got as far as the Bus Stop chicane before locking a front brake and spinning. 'It was my fault,' he said of a rare driving error. When he made the pits he caught a random scrutineering check, which scotched his chances of improvement. In the race he drove superbly as he pulled up to fourth place behind Schumacher, Häkkinen, and Ralf Schumacher, but then the fuel pressure took a dive (or he ran out of fuel, depending who you asked) and he was through for the day. Fastest lap was scant consolation as he was forced to watch his championship chances receding through no real fault of his own.

Italy is always important for Ferrari, and yet again Schumacher grabbed the limelight with pole position and victory, but in qualifying Barrichello was every bit as bright a star, taking second place on the grid only 0.027s slower than Michael. But where Schumacher scored yet another win (and broke down emotionally at the press conference as his tally now matched the late Ayrton Senna's 41) Barrichello had another disappointment, and a narrow escape as he was involved in one of two horrible accidents on the approach to Variante della Roggia, the second chicane, on the opening lap.

According to Heinz-Harald Frentzen, who was following him closely, Barrichello braked earlier than he had expected, catching him unawares. The Jordan driver was planning two pits stops and was running a lighter fuel load than the Ferrari, which may have been a contributory factor. As Frentzen tried to avoid the Ferrari's rear end he collided with teammate Jarno Trulli and both yellow cars spun into Barrichello as he entered the chicane.

Tragically, debris from Frentzen's car struck and killed marshal Paolo Ghislimberti.

Barrichello had impact marks all over his helmet and was very agitated afterwards, publicly accusing Frentzen of rash behaviour and calling for him to be banned. 'What he did was completely unacceptable,' the normally placid Brazilian said, evidently very shaken. The stewards decided it was a racing accident, albeit a tragic one, and Frentzen later censured Barrichello gently when he said: 'In his situation I can understand the feelings, especially driving a Ferrari at Monza, but as he well knows the reasons for any accident are not as simple as he would want everyone to believe.'

America was back on the calendar that year, on a new track situated within the famed Indianapolis Motor Speedway, home of the Indy 500. Here yet again Schumacher was the man in the spotlight, as a stunning victory, and the failure of Häkkinen's McLaren to finish, took him within one final step of the world title. Barrichello followed him home after leap-frogging ahead of Frentzen in the final pit stops, albeit more than 12 seconds adrift, as Ferrari further cemented its control over the constructors' championship with only two races remaining. Schumacher would win both from pole. His success in Japan was sufficient to clinch him his first title with Ferrari as he beat Häkkinen, and it had been made clear from on high to both their teammates that they were not – repeat not – to get in the way of the title fight. In the end, Coulthard beat Barrichello to third place by nine seconds. In Malaysia, Schumacher beat Coulthard to the line by seven-tenths of a second, leaving Barrichello to overcome a dose of flu and a baulky first gear, which delayed him during his second pit stop, to pick up the final podium spot of the year after a strong performance.

The result brought the Brazilian's points tally to 62, giving him easily the best season of his Formula One career, but one pole position and one win looked less impressive against Schumacher's cache of nine poles and nine wins on his way to

108 points in a similar car. It was the first time in his Formula One career that Barrichello had not had the upper hand over his teammate.

As he reflected on this, Barrichello finally had the scale of the mountain ahead of him fixed firmly in his mind. It had been a brave thing to do, to go to Ferrari in the first place. But he had no doubt he had done the right thing even though it was clear that he had met his match and needed to improve his game.

'In the beginning I found it extremely difficult because I had to get used to the team and to form the right relationships with people who had been working with Michael for four years. But I'm proud of what I have been able to accomplish here, and of some of the things I have done to the car in terms of set-up, with the engineers and the technicians. And of course I am proud of my first victory, which helped to make up for the difficult times that I've had this year. Michael is a fantastic driver. We all know that. But next year I am going to keep doing everything that I can to beat him.'

Support for his cause came from no less a figure than Ferrari's technical director Ross Brawn, who told *Autocourse* annual: 'We've got the best reference point you could have. You can see what Michael can do, and it's very easy to dismiss his teammates, even though they may be very, very good. Rubens has done an excellent job. There have been slight inconsistencies, which will disappear. He has been learning to work with the team and we have been discovering what he needs. Once or twice we have made wrong moves; once or twice he has not been able to get it together with the team. Monaco wasn't great, for example. And he struggled at Imola. But we are starting to understand why. Rubens is a good guy to work with and he has settled in well; he's very open and relaxed in the debriefs with Michael in all the discussions we have about what the car is doing – which is essential for the good working of the team.'

Chapter 9

DISAPPOINTMENT
ALLEY, 2001

If ever there was to be a reminder to Rubens Barrichello just how hard life as Michael Schumacher's partner at Ferrari could be, it came in 2001. He finished third in the world championship, behind his illustrious team leader and his super-aggressive old Formula Three foe David Coulthard, but though that was the highest he had ever finished it was a disappointment. A year that promised much ultimately led only to disillusionment.

As far as he was concerned, the year started on a reasonable note in Melbourne. Schumacher took pole position and ran away and hid from him in the race, in which he also set the fastest lap. Coulthard was second and Barrichello came through to take the final podium position, in third place. Coulthard was less than two seconds behind Schumacher's Ferrari, but Barrichello was more than half a minute in arrears. He'd brushed Frentzen's Jordan early in the race, pushing the German into a spin, and as a result the toe-in of his Ferrari was affected for the remainder of the race. By the end his left front Bridgestone was in tatters.

The podium ceremony was muted as Schumacher, Coulthard, and Barrichello were told that marshal Graham Beveridge had been killed by debris after a first lap accident involving Ralf Schumacher and Jacques Villeneuve.

Malaysia saw Schumacher again win from pole position, and once again Barrichello shared the front row with him, a tenth of a second adrift. They led off at the start (itself a restart after Fisichella had wrongly positioned his Renault for the first), but their race was nearly spoiled as a heavy shower turned a dry track into a skating rink. On the third lap both red cars had speared off the treacherous surface, obliging both drivers (and most of their rivals) into the pits for a change of tyres after four laps. As he recovered first Barrichello was the first to reach the pits, so Schumacher had to wait while the Brazilian's car was serviced. They rejoined in 10th and 11th places, Rubens ahead. Ferrari had taken a brilliant tactical decision, however, and put both of its drivers on intermediate tyres rather than full wets. Since the safety car was still circulating (after Olivier Panis's BAR Honda had spun dramatically on lap three), they were simply able to join the back of the pack. This was doubly fortunate, since one of the mechanics had accidentally fitted a full-wet right front tyre on to Barrichello's car before realising his error. As the track began to dry quickly in the tropical conditions, and racing resumed on lap 11, the Ferrari drivers began making up lost ground hand over fist.

By lap 12, when Schumacher moved in front of Barrichello again, they were sixth and seventh, and they worked back into first and second places four laps later. That was where they finished, but for the first time there was tension between them on the podium. Barrichello had been on the radio warning Ross Brawn to warn Michael that there was a lot of dirt on the track, when the champion simply sliced his way by, leaving little room for argument or manoeuvre. Barrichello was distinctly unimpressed.

'It was not what you would expect a teammate to do,' he growled, which was surprising given his relationship with Senna, and some of the tricks he must have been aware the elder Brazilian pulled on teammate Alain Prost in their days together at McLaren. The move, and Barrichello's reaction to it, opened up all over again the debate that he was just too nice a guy to win big in Formula One. 'It's the guys like Schumacher, who are ruthless, who win the big prizes,' one observer remarked.

Barrichello figured the best way to hit back would be to win in Brazil, which was next on the calendar. To his chagrin, however, Schumacher took the pole again, while he could only manage sixth fastest time. He was only four-tenths of a second adrift but the competition was so stiff that somehow there was room for Ralf Schumacher, Häkkinen, Montoya, and Coulthard between the two red cars.

The race was another to be affected partway through by heavy rain, and once Montoya had lost the lead in a collision with backmarker Verstappen on the 38th lap, Coulthard overtook Schumacher in spectacular style to win, with the champion second. There was no fairy story for Barrichello, though, whose race was damned even before the start. As he left the pits for the grid formation laps his engine broke, making it his second failure of the weekend since he'd lost one on Friday, too. It was a hot, muggy day, but all he could do as his enthusiastic fellow countrymen first groaned, then applauded, was run back to the pits for the spare car. This, as usual, was set up for Michael, so while he slumped in the corner of the garage recovering his breath, the mechanics worked frantically to change the pedal set-up and adjust the seat belts as best they could. The pit lane closes 15 minutes before the start of a race, but he just made it out with less than half a minute to spare to take his place on the grid. In the end, however, all the work proved academic. After making a poor start and completing the opening lap in seventh place, he ran into the back of Ralf Schumacher's BMW Williams on the third lap under braking for the first corner. This time the Ferrari's right front wheel was torn off, and his race was most definitely over.

'I was behind Ralf when he suddenly changed line, probably to pass another car, and braked in front of me,' he explained, a trifle sheepishly. 'I did not expect this and the collision was inevitable after that. These things happen in racing ...'

Sceptics thought his adrenaline was still coursing through his veins at a million miles an hour after his problem with his race car, and that he had simply made a misjudgement.

It was Schumacher's turn for retirement at Imola for the San Marino Grand Prix, as his car suffered a brake problem. Barrichello finished third, beaten by Ralf Schumacher (who won his first grand epreuve and thus made himself and Michael the only brothers in history each to have won at this level) and Coulthard. For a while Barrichello lost time trapped behind an unhappy Häkkinen's McLaren, but benefited as his refuelling strategy allowed him to run three laps longer than the Finn in his first stint. This proved crucial, as he was able to pass the McLaren as a result and stay sufficiently clear when they stopped a second time.

In Spain Schumacher got back down to business, taking pole position, winning, and setting fastest lap. Barrichello could only watch and dream. He qualified fourth, jumped up to third behind Schumacher and Häkkinen for the first 23 laps, moving to second as Schumacher refuelled. His own stop two laps later set him back to third, but after his second stop on lap 44 he felt something wrong with the handling, and after an off-course excursion a third pit stop on lap 49 confirmed that something in the rear suspension had broken.

Coulthard rose to the occasion in Austria to take a stylish victory over Michael, with Rubens picking up another podium after starting from fourth place. Coulthard simply stayed out longer than the Ferraris, and took control with one late pit stop, while Barrichello could have been second after Schumacher got into another spat with the emergent Montoya. That day, however, he and the world got a reminder of just what expectations Ferrari had of its second driver.

Montoya led the first 15 laps, with Schumacher eventually deposing his brother to give chase with Rubens keeping him company. On lap 16 Schumacher got a run on Montoya going down to the Remus Kurve, a hairpin with an uphill exit, but as both men braked too late and slid wide Barrichello gratefully pounced into the lead. He held on to it until the 47th lap, when he made his refuelling stop, and this let the longer-running Coulthard into first place. Meanwhile, Schumacher had been recovering and was closing on Barrichello, who was still within spitting distance of the Scot. But Ferrari wanted Schumacher to have the chance, if not to catch the McLaren then at least to minimise the points deficit, and instructed Barrichello to let Schumacher by. It was the Brazilian's first real taste of team orders, Maranello style, but assuredly it would not be his last.

In the final corner he slowed just enough to let Michael by. As Coulthard finished 2.1 seconds ahead of the champion, Barrichello was only three-tenths of a second behind him.

Schumacher had the grace to seem slightly embarrassed afterwards. 'Did I deserve six points today?' he asked. 'Maybe not. But imagine if at the end of the season I lost the world championship by two points.'

Perish the thought.

'Ferrari has a different philosophy and some will disagree with it,' he acknowledged, and though he did not actually say thank you to his teammate, he did add: 'I am very happy he did that,' in recognition of Barrichello's gesture.

The Brazilian is habitually approachable and affable, but that day even these graces were taxed to the limit. After the race he looked gutted. His illustrious teammate, who had already won more races than anyone bar Alain Prost, had slid off the road early in the race through his own error, while he had kept his composure and driven an impeccable race, but it was beginning to dawn upon him that this did not matter as far as Ferrari's management was concerned. As long as it was possible, Schumacher had to be extended every courtesy in the pursuit of success. What the world believed to be a fact, it seemed, Rubens Barrichello was just beginning to appreciate for himself. He was there to help, not to upstage.

Jean Todt said that his dream would have been to see Rubens win in front of David that day, but that since it was only second or third place that was under discussion, he could not see the difference. Barrichello clearly did not share that unusual point of view.

He found it difficult to speak. 'The team ordered me to move over,' he reported, stony-faced. 'I am not happy with the situation. I have very few things to say at this press conference. I need to speak to the team to clarify a few things. Unfortunately I cannot open my heart right now, I'm sorry.'

Loyalty rarely comes any better packaged than that. Barrichello might not have won the race, or even finished second, but his stock was a darn sight higher than Schumacher's in the press room that day.

Schumacher's title challenge had got well under way by that Austrian race, but Monte Carlo marked the point at which it began to hit high gear, and in which Coulthard's hit trouble. The Scot won a brilliant pole position, but an electronics problem caused his McLaren to stall on the grid before the final formation lap, and he was obliged to drop down to the back as the grid reformed. This suited Schumacher perfectly as he started from the other front row position. Apart from the five laps that Barrichello enjoyed in the lead – 55 to 59, while Schumacher refuelled – the champion had no need to rely on his partner's generosity, as he simply dominated. Barrichello, by contrast, spent the first 12 laps studying the rear end of Häkkinen's McLaren until the silver car headed to the pits with handling problems, and thereafter he ran comfortably behind Schumacher all the way to the flag. As the latter backed off in the final stages, they finished less than half a second apart. It was not an easy result, however, as the Brazilian suffered bad cramp in his right foot.

'It started around lap three and was really bad,' he revealed. 'I started asking Ross if there was anything I could do in the cockpit to help. He was like a physiotherapist!'

Since it was the right foot, and unlike Schumacher he did not like left-foot braking and therefore relied on the right both to accelerate and slow the car, this was a serious problem.

'Ross kept telling me to drink water and that helped, but I was having quite a few problems.'

If there was a consolation, it was that Ferrari announced officially that it had renewed his contract for 2002. Nobody said whether this was done early as a sweetener for the disappointment he suffered in Austria.

Canada and the Grand Prix of Europe at the Nürburgring both proved disappointing. As Schumacher finished second from pole in Montreal, and then won from pole in Germany, Barrichello had only a retirement and a fifth place to celebrate. While Michael initially led brother Ralf round the Ile Notre Dame in Montreal, Barrichello climbed from fifth on the grid to third and was fighting a traction control problem as he homed in on Schumacher Jnr. But as he exited the hairpin on lap six he spun, dropping down to 14th place. 'I'd switched the traction control off on lap three,' he admitted. 'Whatever the problem was, it was causing a misfire and that was what cased my spin.'

Still struggling with the behaviour of his car, he began chasing after Montoya's BMW Williams. They were running 10th and 11th by lap 19, but as they sped nose-to-tail through the fast sweeps by the old Olympic rowing basin towards the end of the lap, Montoya put a wheel in the dirt and spun and Barrichello had to spin into retirement trying to avoid him.

The BMW Williams duo again got between the Ferrari drivers during qualifying at the Nürburgring, where Michael took pole from his brother and Montoya with Barrichello fourth. Right from the start Rubens was in trouble, slumping down to seventh place and giving himself a mountain to climb as he contended with serious tyre vibrations in his first stint. By the time he got a better set of Bridgestones it was too late to do anything, and he had to be satisfied with only two points.

It was becoming a source of discouragement for Barrichello that his teammate led such a seemingly charmed life. But even though Michael stormed from pole to yet another win at Magny-Cours in the French Grand Prix, Rubens had the consolation of driving a snorter of a race after clever strategy helped him to move forward after he could only qualify eighth, complaining that his car felt nervous under braking and needed a new front suspension torsion bar after he'd walloped a kerb. During his first stint Ross Brawn suggested they switch him to a three-stop refuelling strategy, and on a track where overtaking is notoriously difficult this worked perfectly to bring him four points and the final podium place after a worthy afternoon's effort.

The French race presaged a solid run for Barrichello as the summer progressed. There was another third at Silverstone in the British Grand Prix, followed by seconds (to Ralf and Michael respectively) in Germany and Hungary.

Long stints between refuelling paid off at Silverstone, and he was pleased with a podium at the circuit where so much of his formative life in Europe had been spent, but he never felt completely comfortable with the Ferrari's balance. 'I was driving carefully while trying to be quick!' he confessed.

Germany was the scene of a massive shunt for fellow countryman Luciano Burti as his Prost slammed into Michael's ailing Ferrari and was launched into the air at the start of the race. On the restart Schumacher took the spare car, which quit on him with a fuel pressure problem. Incredibly, as these words were written in January 2005 that marked the last time the German dropped out of a race through mechanical reasons…

Barrichello, meanwhile, made a relatively poor start but soon moved up to fourth place. He then passed Michael, and when Montoya lost the lead through engine failure he followed Ralf to the flag. 'Given that we felt the Williams was on another level,' he reported, 'the two-stop strategy was the right decision and I was the only one who could match their pace at the start, thanks to that.' He had particularly enjoyed a close battle with Coulthard, until the Scot's engine blew.

Hungary went Michael's way yet again, with the champion winning from pole and equalling Alain Prost's record of 51 grand prix triumphs in the process. Barrichello qualified third but helped himself enormously at the start by beating second fastest Coulthard into the first corner, so that the red cars ran 1–2. Coulthard chased him hard, but in the end the luck ran his way as he backed Michael up in another perfect race for Ferrari.

So far it had been a very tough season for Barrichello, while Schumacher seemed to walk on water (as usual). He'd put in several excellent drives and the team regarded him as a more rounded performer than Eddie Irvine; but it was a balancing act, being number two at Ferrari. Clearly the fight for the title was over, but with second place still up for grabs, Barrichello had his sights firmly focused.

'I think it's fairly important [to finish second],' he said ironically. 'First place has been taken already. I think the next best is second, so I'm giving it my best. I have four races to win the race. It's not very common for you to see the whole team working for two drivers and you have to have Michael who is someone who can help you, because most of the time he is flat out doing his job and most of the time you're there to help him. So now we have four races and that isn't very common so I have to take the best out of that situation and try to win and basically if I finish second, I will be happier than if I finish third.

'I don't know if Michael will help. I think he said himself to the press that Ferrari wishes to finish one and two and then we would win everything during the year. I said before, if he's winning the race and I'm fourth or fifth or whatever, then there's no way he can help so I have to help myself, but we haven't discussed that, which way he's going to help.'

It had been difficult for him in recent months, and the media in Brazil had been on his case, wanting to know why he wasn't winning races. 'I think Brazil is very critical when talking about anything,' he admitted. 'If Cuertin [the footballer] is winning, he's fantastic. If he's not winning, he's not playing well. It's just like that. It's not something in between. You don't have the support all the time when you need it, but so far they are looking at the position as "Four races to go, Rubens might have a chance to win so let's support him". But during the year there were times when I thought that they shouldn't have said so many things because they cause so much stress, and I think the public doesn't deserve that. I think that the public is just there to cheer it up and sometimes they have false information, which is bad.

'As far as I'm concerned, the season has just started. I think it's a great fight with David and Ralf and I saw a lot of people with the number one cap for Michael, saying, "Rubens! Rubens!" It's just starting for me.'

In the end, he lost the fight with Coulthard, 65 points to 56. Spa ultimately brought only fifth place, as would Japan, the season finale. At the Belgian circuit, while Schumacher set a new record by scoring an untroubled 52nd win, Barrichello made a rare driving error and lost time and places and his chance of a podium finish when he took off his front wing on one of the plastic markers in the dreaded Bus Stop chicane, and had to do a slow lap without the wing before he could pit for a new one. It certainly didn't help that Coulthard finished second.

In Japan he was almost a second off polesitter Schumacher as he qualified fourth, but jumped quickly up to challenge Montoya for second place as he tried to make the most of a light fuel load. He and Ferrari figured his only chance of winning was to run light early on with a three-stop refuelling strategy, try to build an advantage, and then make quick enough stops to maintain it. His move on Ralf Schumacher in the challenging 130R left-hander should have been sufficient to convince even his greatest critic that he is a proper racer, and then he outbraked Montoya into the chicane on the second lap and was briefly second over the line, but when the Colombian had sufficient momentum to drag by again by the first corner his big chance of second place in the title race had gone. 'It's disappointing,' was all he said later.

In between, he was classified 15th at Indianapolis but was not running at the end after his engine broke after 71 of the 73 laps. This was particularly cruel fortune, as he had led laps five to 26, after passing first Montoya and then Schumacher, and laps 46 to 49 after his first pit stop, and following his second he was pushing hard after leader Häkkinen and running ahead of Michael. 'If nothing else,' he shrugged, 'today shows that having the spare car at my disposal proves the team believes in the fact I can win, and I showed that I have the right motivation to succeed in that.'

Of the four races, Monza was the best, and with better fortune he should have won there. Instead, he finished a strong second only five seconds away from winner Montoya.

Monza is traditionally a happy weekend, for the Italians embody the very spirit and passion that have made motorsport what it is today. But that September weekend there were no smiles, for the atrocity of the Twin Towers in New York was fresh and raw in every mind and for once a sport of vested interest and personal ambition was united in its condemnation of terrorist activities and the threat they pose to any civilised society. The two Schumacher brothers in particular were off-colour all weekend, each believing that they might be a target for possible terrorist attack as the forces of Al Qaeda were credited with almost mythical power in the wake of the destruction of so many lives in Manhattan. There was even talk that the race might be cancelled, but in the end carrying on with normality was deemed to be the best response. Both Ferraris ran with carbon black noses as a mark of respect.

This was one of the few occasions on which Schumacher could be said to have delivered less than his best. Then came another awful setback with the news on Saturday afternoon that, over at the Lausitzring in Germany, which earlier in the year had claimed the life of popular ex-Formula One star Michele Alboreto, the equally well-liked Alex Zanardi had suffered a terrible accident in the CART race which had severed both of his legs. If possible, the mood in the paddock darkened even further.

Montoya grabbed pole position in his BMW Williams, but Barrichello was right there alongside him, only three-tenths adrift and a tenth ahead of Michael.

Avoiding carnage in the first chicane thanks to being ahead of it, Barrichello hounded Montoya round the opening lap. Ferrari had gone for two refuelling stops, BMW Williams one, so it was imperative that he overtake in order to make optimum use of his lighter fuel load. He stayed in Montoya's slipstream until he saw his opportunity on lap nine as Montoya blistered a tyre because of the greater weight of his fuel load. Now Barrichello surged clear as Schumacher moved up to challenge for second place. Barrichello was 9.5 seconds ahead when he made his first pit stop on lap 19, a lap later than Schumacher. Judging by the champion's stop, Barrichello should have been standing still for no more than 10 seconds, but instead the Ferrari was stationary for an agonising 16.3 seconds. Unfortunately a problem had arisen as the mechanics recalibrated the rig. It is a heavy unit and had to be manhandled away while they changed the calibration from Schumacher's heavier load to the lighter one that had been planned for Barrichello. The job was done with commendable speed in the circumstances, but the delay was sufficient to deny him any hope of victory. And he was further hampered because now more fuel than intended had been put into the tank, so the car was not as fast as the two-stop strategy demanded.

After finishing only 5.17 seconds behind Montoya, who he was confident he would otherwise have beaten, Barrichello displayed his loyalty to the team.

'For sure the two-stop strategy was definitely the right decision,' he said. 'Ross was magic to think of this, which gave us the chance to fight the Williams. I am not sure what happened in the pit stop, but it cost me a lot of time. Enough to lose the race.'

Ultimately, then, 2001 was a year of disappointment. Disappointment at failing to win a race; disappointment at failing to finish second in the championship; disappointment at failing to match Schumacher sufficiently. Once again the champion had taken nine victories from 11 poles, and on the way to his fourth world title he scored 123 points. This time Barrichello did worse than he had in 2000, finishing only third without poles or victories and with 56 points, six fewer than he had scored the previous season.

But he was further seasoned, and this time Brawn told *Autocourse*: 'You know where you are with Rubens; he wears his heart on his sleeve. He's never been malicious. He's got emotionally upset and disagreed with the team, but that's always been the end of it. If we've got a bad car then Rubens is just as capable as Michael of getting a decent race out of it. But over one lap Michael has the edge.'

In terms of the overall result, finishing third in the championship, he had climbed to another stage on his personal Everest, but on 2001 form there seemed little prospect that he would enjoy the view from the top that Michael Schumacher seemed determined to make his own special preserve.

Chapter 10

ORDER, ORDER, ORDER! 2002

If there were times in 2001 when Rubens Barrichello felt like an outsider in his own team, they were nothing compared to what lay ahead in 2002, a year in which Ferrari engineered far and away the greatest car in the field. It won 15 of the 17 grands prix. In his days at Stewart Ford it was what Barrichello would have salivated for, a technical advantage that enabled him to worry more about what he was doing in the cockpit than what anyone else was doing on the track.

As things transpired, and Ferrari won its fourth consecutive world championship for constructors with such imperious ease that its points tally of 221 more than doubled immediate rival Williams's score (92), it would deliver to him his best-ever drivers' title position: second. But again the success was bitter-sweet. He had never before scored 77 points in a season, nor as many as four grand prix victories. But Michael Schumacher was again the world champion, and he won 11 of the races and scored 144 points, almost double Barrichello's tally.

Worse than that, much worse, some of Barrichello's 'victories' were not victories at all, they were gifts from the man alongside whom he drove, and who, for the second year running, had denied him his rightful win in Austria on a remarkable day when the Brazilian had clearly had his measure.

Instead of the glory that was rightfully his that day, he had to step aside, and when he won in the future, notably at the Hungaroring and Indianapolis, he was made to look foolish by a teammate who, clumsily, thought he was doing the right thing.

While all that brought ferocious criticism upon the heads of Schumacher and the architect of it all, sporting director Jean Todt, there was a further sting in the tail for Barrichello. As if his position was not sufficiently untenable (barring his healthy income, estimated around $12 million annually), he was criticised by his detractors in the media for lacking the balls to throw it back in Ferrari's face and stick out for his rightful results. But he could not do that without the danger of being shown the door. And who would want to risk that? More than anything, 2002 was a reminder for the now 30-year-old from Sao Paulo that he had been responsible for making the bed he now found himself forced to sleep in.

As usual, the season got off to a better start for Michael than it did for Rubens. The champion won the Australian Grand Prix in Melbourne, after Barrichello had demonstrated that the fire still burned by taking pole position ahead of him, albeit by a margin of only 0.005 seconds.

'I think things happen in life for a reason,' he said afterwards. 'I think it's a very good beginning of the year. I've done good testing. I feel relaxed. I think I've changed the approach of everything so I feel good, actually. But this qualifying means, for sure, it is good to be starting tomorrow in pole position but it was only two runs and then it rained – actually the rain so many times has helped me in my life so this time it helped me too, so it was a bit up in the air, to be honest. We know our car is competitive. Michael would have gone faster, I feel I would have gone faster, but it's good to be here.'

His first run had been spoiled by traffic, but he had been shrewd enough to bang in a second quick run just before the rain arrived with a vengeance. If there was luck involved, he had made his own. But still he insisted: 'I don't think I've been right or wrong today. I think everybody knew that it could get wet. I set my first time but I got traffic and there were yellow flags all around, and then we decided to go for another time because it looked like getting tricky, the weather just spinning out. Even when we were running since the beginning, there were some dark clouds and some spitting on the visor, so we just decided to go and give it one more try.'

The first race of the season is the one where everyone seems mellow, chilled out after the winter break, buoyed by the promise of pre-season testing. Barrichello looked no different to his habitual self, grinning broadly and talking to anyone. But there was little doubt that the pole had done him good, helped him to relax even more.

'It's a tough life just to be number two to Michael,' he volunteered, 'and there a lot of questions involving him and sometimes you are not happy because of a small thing and it becomes a big thing in the press, so I just said that this year I'm not going to bother any more. I just said I would stop crying – if that's what I was doing – and just get on with the job and enjoy it, because at the end of the day we have to remember why I do this. It's because I love it and it seems that it's working. I'm particularly driving better than ever and it's a good time for myself just to enjoy and drive the car.'

The car in question was a heavily updated version of the 2001 Ferrari, whereas all of the team's rivals had gone for new cars. Ferrari's own F2002 had already been tested, but was being held back until the start of the European season in April. Old or new, Barrichello was very happy with what the team had given him.

'From the outside it doesn't look different at all. But Bridgestone has done a fantastic job so we made it very suitable, set-up wise, for the tyre. Engine-wise, I think we have more power, some small touches on the electronics and this and that, and the fact that we know the car so well and we can go to the extreme with this set-up and things like this, that's the reason why we're faster.'

It wasn't speed that was Barrichello's concern come race day, however. It was more a case of shedding it. The moment the race began he jumped into the lead, with Ralf Schumacher pushing through to beat brother Michael into the first corner, a slow right/left chicane. When the field arrived there, all hell broke loose and Michael was perfectly positioned to watch his brother's BMW Williams leap skywards after crashing into and over the back of Barrichello's Ferrari. Fortunately nobody was hurt, but the incident also accounted for Allan McNish's Toyota, Olivier Panis's BAR Honda, the Renaults of Jenson Button and Giancarlo Fisichella, and Nick Heidfeld's Sauber Petronas. Ralf blamed Barrichello for braking sooner than expected; Barrichello blamed Ralf for braking too late.

'I had a great start, and got Michael easily,' Schumacher Jnr said. 'I wanted to pass Barrichello too, so I tried the inside and he closed the door, I then went to the outside and he closed it again. I made my last attempt going to the inside and he closed the door and braked at the same time. I cannot complain about the braking, as we were going into the first corner, even if I thought it was a bit early, but he definitely changed direction twice and we are only allowed to do it once.'

'I was trying to defend my position as we went into the braking area,' Barrichello countered, 'and then of course I had to brake. I don't think I did it too early. In fact I think, quite the opposite. I braked later than usual as I was worried something like this might happen. It was a heavy impact and I reckon Ralf was flat out. I don't think he would have got round the corner.'

Michael took a middle line. 'Obviously it was ideal from my point of view, but from Rubens's point of view it didn't go so well,' he said, and was there just a hint of censure when he added: 'It would have been better for two of us to be at the finish rather than just the one.'

That opening race tended to set the tone for the first half of Barrichello's year, as disaster followed disaster. Ralf Schumacher scored a rare victory for BMW Williams and Michelin in the heat of Malaysia, where his big brother took pole and finished third. Michael then won in Brazil, driving the only Ferrari F2002. Both races brought further retirements and despair for Barrichello, whose title aspirations had all but evaporated with Schumacher's healthy tally of 24 points to his zero. In Malaysia his engine broke while he was lying second behind Ralf, leaving him distraught; at home his F2001 suffered hydraulic failure after 16 laps, three laps after he had taken the lead from Michael thanks to running a different refuelling strategy.

'I just think it is like golf,' he shrugged. 'You play a bad hole on the first one, you have got to think it is going to be better on the second one. If the second one is still bad you have got to think the third is better. So I am on that. The fourth one has to be better so I am positive about it, but I am not too concerned about the bad luck I have had.'

San Marino was an important event for Ferrari, as it brought the team back to Europe and home ground. Michael parked his on pole, with Rubens alongside him less than a tenth of a second adrift in an F2002 of his own. But behind those facts lies a story: such was Barrichello's pace that Schumacher first had to copy his chassis set-up, then actually commandeer his car, in order to match him.

The race belonged to Schumacher, however, but this time Barrichello was second 18s adrift and had the consolation of fastest lap as the Scuderia's rivals finally got a genuine indication of just how tough a challenge they faced. The Brazilian's only problem came when old Jordan teammate Eddie Irvine got in his way while his Jaguar was being lapped. 'I'd like to tell him to go to hell!' Barrichello growled with unusual anger.

Spain brought yet another win for Schumacher, who also started from pole and set fastest lap. But Barrichello, though he had once again qualified on the front row, didn't even take part. His Ferrari stayed resolutely on the grid as the final formation lap began, before being wheeled into retirement with an electronic problem that denied him any gears.

Austria seemed set to make up for all that, as for the second year in succession he had clear superiority over Schumacher. But instead the race would be yet one more demoralising event. By now Schumacher had 44 points. Juan Pablo Montoya was next on 23 followed by Ralf Schumacher with 20. After that David Coulthard had nine, Jenson Button eight, and Barrichello six. Unless somebody could teach pigs to aviate, it seemed unlikely that anyone was seriously going to challenge the German on his way to matching Juan Manuel Fangio's five world championships, but there was always the outside chance that BMW Williams and/or Michelin might suddenly come good.

Qualifying went well for Barrichello. With far more confidence than he might have been expected to demonstrate given his results thus far, he lapped in 1m 08.082s, heading Ralf Schumacher with 1m 08.364s. Unusually Michael was only third, on 1m 08.704s. It transpired that much of the cause for Barrichello's cheerfulness was a new contract which would take him through to the end of 2004.

There was a story behind that, emanating from a suggestion in the British press that he had been forced to accept a pay cut. 'It is such bullshit that it is not even worth comment,' he reacted angrily. 'Ferrari keeps me because they love me racing the car, so if they don't like me to be here they are going to tell me to go home or to go and find another team. But a pay cut because of what? What did I do wrong? In the first three races I was leading, in fact, when I had my problems. I never told my salary, so nobody is going to ever know anyway.'

Barrichello swept confidently into the lead, with Michael quickly moving to second ahead of fast-starting Nick Heidfeld in a Ferrari-engined Sauber Petronas, and brother Ralf. After 20 laps, Ralf was half a minute behind after passing Heidfeld. The two Ferraris remained in control though until they both came into the pits on the 24th lap for opportunistic first pit stops after the safety car had been deployed the previous lap as Panis's BAR spun on the pit straight following engine failure. Barrichello resumed in the lead, but Schumacher Jnr, on a single-stop strategy, moved to second ahead of his sibling. The safety car came out again almost immediately, when Heidfeld and Takuma Sato in a Jordan were involved in a frightening collision.

Right the way through to his second stop on lap 61, however, Barrichello held a commanding lead even after Michael moved back into second place on the 47th lap when Ralf finally refuelled. It seemed all over bar the shouting: the Brazilian was headed for the second – and by far the better – victory of his Formula One career.

But ...

In the pits, television cameras caught Jean Todt hovering anxiously. Surely the Ferrari manager could not be considering doing to Barrichello what he had done to him at the same venue the previous year?

Even as Barrichello and Schumacher swept into the final lap, that issue was in doubt. Rubens still had a second over Michael. But several laps earlier Todt had begun instructing him over the radio to let Michael by. In the cockpit poor Barrichello simply could not believe that the team was asking him to do the same thing all over again, especially when Schumacher had such a clear points advantage and Ferrari had such an unchallenged technical upper hand. But Todt *was* asking precisely that even though Barrichello was holding a four-second lead, and having begun asking around the 61st lap, he stopped asking and began telling as the 71st and final lap approached.

'This is one of the occasions we will have to ask you to move over,' was Todt's opening gambit, and out on the track Schumacher seemed so confident that Barrichello would comply (or else had resigned himself to second place) that he was making no obvious effort to close the gap.

In the end, Barrichello kept Todt waiting until the very last moment, before very pointedly slowing down after the final corner to let his teammate steal his win. The crowd exploded in a fury of booing and catcalling, and as it dawned on the Todt-Brawn-Schumacher triumvirate just how deeply unpopular a decision it had been, the champion effected to be surprised by Barrichello's action, and compounded the embarrassment Rubens must have been feeling by pushing him on to the top step of the podium. It was a hollow gesture that merely provoked the crowd further, throwing a very large egg on to the erubescent face of Austria's chancellor, Dr Wolfgang Schussel, who was the dignitary tasked with dishing out the trophies.

Subsequently Ferrari was summoned by the FIA to explain itself and much fuss would be made about the whole thing by the governing body and the media, but in the final analysis not much really changed.

Meanwhile, Schumacher was left to try and bluff out an angry press conference, as an emotional Barrichello tried hard to maintain his composure.

Earlier in the year he had responded carefully to suggestions in Brazil, since picked up and magnified by the Italian media, that he was prepared to leave Ferrari if it ever gave a new car only to his teammate and made him do with an older model. In denying them he gave a clear insight into his stance within the team.

'I have no problems with Ferrari. I have no problems with anything. I'm entitled to my opinion. I sit down with Ross and Jean, we talk and by no means am I a man of no opinion. I have my opinion. I race to win and sometimes you are and sometimes you're not happy. Right now I'm a happy man with Ferrari.'

But that was then and this was now, and this wound hurt desperately. 'I would rather not say anything right now,' he said. 'I apologise because I know that you want to hear what I have to say, but I think it is best that I keep my feelings on this to myself.'

It was a more dignified response than anyone at Ferrari deserved, and another telling indication of the character within the Brazilian's unhappy frame.

'I cannot ask everyone to agree with our decision,' an unrepentant Todt said. 'But it is our decision. We are only at one-third distance in the championship and two years ago we had three retirements in a row.'

Unpopular though his decision was, Todt had to look at things from a different perspective from enthusiasts with nothing greater, perhaps, than an emotional investment in the overall well-being of a major race team, but he shovelled away any ground he might have made up with that statement when he attempted to suggest: 'Rubens was the moral winner, but he offered the victory to Michael for the interests of the championship. Whether it was right or wrong is another matter. But it may be that by the end of the season people will see it as the right thing to do.'

Some three years later, Todt's detractors showed no sign of changing their initial stance.

David Coulthard stormed to a great victory in Monaco, with Schumacher second, but the best that a troubled Barrichello could do was seventh with fastest lap after a tough afternoon. Starting fifth, he would be penalised twice, the first time for crashing into the back of Kimi Räikkönen's McLaren, the second for speeding in the pit lane. 'I spotted a chance to pass Räikkönen, I went from the outside to the inside, and he closed the door on me,' he said. 'There was nothing I could do, but I have to thank the team for building a really strong car. But it's a race to forget, because I had a winning car this afternoon.'

Finally, things began to pick up again in Canada, where he led for the first 25 laps, but ultimately Schumacher's single-stop strategy proved superior to his two stops because his own opening stint had been hurt by the intervention of the safety car after Jacques Villeneuve's BAR Honda had stopped on a dangerous part of the circuit. He finished third, separated from the victorious German by Coulthard, who had to employ all sorts of tactics to keep him at bay. It was another race he finished with mounting frustration.

Finally, the tears flowed for the right reasons after the Grand Prix of Europe at the Nürburgring. He started this one from fourth on the grid on a rare occasion when BMW Williams elbowed Ferrari off the front row, but led every lap, shadowed home by his teammate, who had spun early on. This time, Ferrari dare not invoke any team orders, as it was due to answer for its Austrian wiles to the FIA World Motorsport Council in Paris three days later.

'Is this payback for Austria?' Barrichello asked. 'That was in the past. That time, the strategy favoured Michael, this time it went in my favour. It shows what a strong united group we are.'

The critics took that to mean he had sold out and accepted a minion's role, but he wasn't interested in their views. 'Now I want to enjoy today as my son and wife are both here and it has been a fantastic day,' he said, and that was that. Win number two finally delivered, coincidentally also on German soil.

Ferrari travelled to Britain for the grand prix at Silverstone half a million dollars lighter. The World Motorsport Council had fined it one million for disrupting the podium in Austria, but half the fine was suspended for 12 months. Many felt that a team as wealthy as the Scuderia had got off lightly. Barrichello couldn't care less. That was history. He was much more concerned with showing off his tee-shirt with the 2–0 on it, an indication of Brazil's World Cup success over Germany. If he had a beef, it was that he had not yet been able to get hold of Michael by 'phone to wind him up.

The team had the last laugh that weekend, finishing 1–2 with Michael 14 seconds clear of Rubens in slippery conditions. The Brazilian might have made more of a race of it had he not suffered a last-minute electronics glitch which obliged him to start from the back of the grid and drive superbly to snatch six more points. With the season just past its halfway point the title was clearly going Schumacher's way, but Barrichello was making ground and had moved up to second with 32, a point ahead of Montoya whom he beat into third place.

Incredibly, he failed to start a grand prix for the second time in the season in France, where Schumacher won yet again once upstart Räikkönen had spun on oil, and clinched his fifth championship title amid great emotion. Once again the second Ferrari suffered electronic gremlins which even a change of steering wheel failed to solve. Barrichello left early and had boarded his private jet at Nevers' local airstrip when the news came through of Schumacher's double triumph. It says everything about the Brazilian that he decamped and went back to the circuit, so he could offer his own congratulations as the celebrations continued into the night.

'I was on the plane and ready to go,' he admitted. 'But we are a family and we stick together through thick and thin.' Small wonder insiders at Ferrari rate him so highly as a man.

Just to keep the party going Schumacher next won on his home ground at Hockenheim, delighting his fans with a triple slam of pole, victory, and fastest lap. Barrichello took fourth behind the BMW Williams duo. And, yet again, his car played up at the start, refusing to upshift. This time he just managed to sprint back for the spare, and he just got out of the pits before the pit lane closed. This time he made it by a quarter of a minute, half the time he'd made it by in Brazil the previous year. Even this drama should not have held him back to fourth, but as he was battling Schumacher Jnr he suffered a problem with his refuelling rig, which dropped him from podium contention.

His luck, however, was finally about to change for the better. He put his F2002 on pole ahead of Schumacher at the Hungarian Grand Prix. 'Rubens did a good job today and I could not match it,' Schumacher allowed, somewhat sportingly it seemed, since he was only 0.061 seconds short.

If there was a payback for Austria, this seemed to be it as Barrichello stormed to victory ahead of Schumacher on the day that the team's 11th win of the year and its fifth 1–2 was sufficient to clinch a fourth consecutive constructors' title. Again Rubens led throughout, with the sole exception of Ralf Schumacher's one lap in the lead at the 33-lap mark as Barrichello refuelled. But Michael stalked him throughout as the two red cars enjoyed a race of their own before finishing nose-to-tail. Their lap times were all over the place as they cruised, and Schumacher showed exactly what they had been up to when he reduced a four second deficit by 3.2 seconds on the final lap.

'Today was a fantastic feeling with a great car, great pit stops and great everything!' Barrichello beamed, celebrating win number three, and suddenly the Austrian incident seemed a long, long way away.

He came down to earth at Spa, as Michael won from pole and set fastest lap and Rubens had to be content with second again, having run different tyres, two seconds behind. 'It would have been too much to ask for us to change positions,' Barrichello said, perhaps slightly tongue in cheek, before adding: 'I think he deserved today. He was so dominant this weekend and it was clear after three or four laps that I could not follow him as I had too many blisters on the front tyres. Michael was in a different league today.'

It was another interesting little insight, into their relationship and into their respective abilities.

But then came Monza, and victory number four. Montoya beat them all to pole, setting a new outright qualifying record of 161.499mph in the process. Initially his teammate Ralf Schumacher led him, with Barrichello and Schumacher Snr chasing along behind. But by lap six Ralf had deliberately dropped back to avoid a penalty for shooting the first chicane on the opening lap and Montoya had broken his car's suspension, so the red cars were in charge. Rubens was on a two-stop strategy, and Michael one, and somewhere in all the maths Michael managed to stay behind his teammate as Jean Todt and Ross Brawn cleverly orchestrated another 'race' between their drivers.

'To be honest, I was confused because I didn't know what was happening,' Barrichello said of the moment the race opened up to him and he took the lead on lap six. 'I just saw a moment there and all of a sudden I saw Ralf slowing down a little bit and I dived on the inside and I was able to get the slipstream off Montoya as well, so I had a perfect lap when I came up from third to first ... The car was getting better and better, so I was really able to push fast and do my race.'

While enthusing about the tyre that Bridgestone had provided – 'It was unbelievable. From the test last week to now it was just the tyre to have!' – Barrichello joined Schumacher in savouring the moment on the podium in front of the adoring *tifosi*. Perhaps they also enjoyed having their former teammate Eddie Irvine there for company, after one of Jaguar's few good races.

'All the way down the straight, and it's by far the longest straight, you see it just full of people,' Schumacher said. 'Full of the *tifosi*, and that's an amazing emotion that went through me and Rubens.'

'Michael called my attention to it,' Barrichello said. 'I don't think we are ever going to experience something like that again. As far as my eyes could go I saw only people, it was amazing.'

There were plenty of them at Indianapolis, too, but there the spectators could scarcely believe what they saw at the end of the US Grand Prix as the Ferraris crossed the finish line side-by-side. Who had won? Schumacher, who seemed to have the race in the bag? Or Barrichello, who seemed to falter then surge ahead at the last moment?

The official nod went to Barrichello, perhaps as Michael had intended, but only by 0.011 seconds. As theatrical moments in motorsport go, it was not the best choreographed by any means.

These are the facts: Michael led every lap apart from 27 and 28 after his first refuelling stop, 49 and 50 after his second, and 73. Rubens, by contrast, dogged him all the way and led on the laps after Michael had refuelled. Schumacher was attempting to stage a dead heat, or so he said, and having asked the team if he could do it he was told no. Doubtless Todt was mindful of more official ire and penalties. But coming out of the final corner Schumacher slowed anyway to let Barrichello alongside. Slowed is of course a relative term, but things were complicated by Barrichello's conscience.

'As I saw Michael go wide and slow down, I was not sure whether he was trying to give me the race or whether he was in trouble, in which case I did not want to take advantage.' Across the road, in the other cockpit, Schumacher was frantically willing him to go by without having to signal. Finally Barrichello got the message, and the deed was done.

'It took me three-quarters of a lap to understand if I had won or not, because I was pointing to him and he was pointing to me. I didn't know if I had won the race or not,' he admitted later.

The Americans went mad.

Far from seeing it as one teammate paying back another's good deeds, many saw it as a betrayal of all the fans, not the least those who might have had a bet on the German winning. The whole thing backfired badly.

'I know a lot of people won't understand a staged finish, but we were trying to do it side-by-side,' Schumacher said as he attempted to explain the latest controversy in his lengthy career. And gesturing towards Barrichello, he added: 'It is difficult for people to appreciate how much I had to fight to keep this guy behind me today.'

Rubens merely tried to say the right things, while looking distinctly bemused.

American journalist Lewis Franck, of the *Monterey County Herald*, told *Motoring News*: 'Speaking on behalf of the average American fan, we don't understand this result.

'It's akin to taking a dive in boxing, and that's manipulating the outcome of a result. And that's not done here, that's not fair play in the USA. You don't take a dive.

'When Austria happened there was absolute outrage amongst sporting people – especially motor racing fans.

'Here Jean Todt said the outcome is the same whoever won. But if this was college sport, forget it. They would get kicked out of the sporting association.'

Ferrari's quite remarkable year of domination ended in Japan, with another 1–2. This time, however, there was no doubt about the winner, as Schumacher triumphed from pole and set fastest lap, and Barrichello brought his F2002 home in his wheeltracks as Michael backed off in the closing laps.

So 11-time winner Schumacher either broke (or in the case of the number of world titles, equalled) all the records. But how you ultimately viewed the 2002 season depended on who you were. If you were a Ferrari fan, or a Michael Schumacher fan, or if you made your living from either, you were doubtless delirious. Certainly Schumacher had no complaints as he matched the great Juan Manuel Fangio's five titles, and neither did Jean Todt as Ferrari won its fourth constructors' title in a row. But it helped the latter that he had a thick skin. More than anyone, he was torn apart by the critics who accused him of dictatorial behaviour that was detrimental to the sport's image and integrity. His response, always given calmly but with his trademark hint of steeliness, was that his job was to do the best for Ferrari, not for the sport. And such is the pressure of a multi-million dollar game that he could not altogether be blamed for doing what he was paid (handsomely) to do.

If you were a casual fan of the sport or, worse still, a purist, 2002 was agony, a season in which one team not only dominated the racing but saw fit to jiggle it around and to control who won, and where. It wasn't the first time team orders had dictated races. Mercedes-Benz had long used such tactics; Denny Hulme and Ken Miles were cheated out of their rightful victory at Le Mans in 1966 by Ford politics; Ferrari actually staged a dead heat between Mike Parkes and Lodovico Scarfiotti in the non-championship Syracuse Grand Prix in 1967; Lotus had employed team orders in 1978 to prevent prodigal son Ronnie Peterson challenging Mario Andretti at times. More recently, David Coulthard had been threatened by radio with the sack if he did not slow up and let teammate Mika Häkkinen score his maiden GP victory in Jerez in 1997, and at other times he had to let the Finn by. But never had such tactics been used so ruthlessly, nor with such complete disregard for the image and well-being of the sport. Either way, a Ferrari won the US GP at Indianapolis when Schumacher gifted the race to Barrichello on the line, but of all the places to choose for such an ill-judged display, America was the least appropriate. The Americans were sceptical about Formula One, they were just beginning to get used to it all over again since its return in 2000 after a lengthy absence. But they don't like races to be contrived (even if they love NASCAR, where the rules are frequently changed to maintain the status quo) and they want to see genuine competition. That race alone did more damage to Formula One's reputation the world over than Ferrari will ever realise.

And if you were Rubens Barrichello... Well, you just had to wonder exactly what kind of contract the Brazilian had signed when he went to join the best team and driver in the game. Like Gerhard Berger and Eddie Irvine before him, at McLaren and Ferrari respectively, he had joined the top team of the day only to discover that the dream was curdled by the presence of a better driver in the other car. And as Irvine had discovered, the better driver at Ferrari had things in place within the team that ensured that he always got prime treatment.

Back in 1988 McLaren Honda had enjoyed such a massive technical advantage that everybody went to every one of the 16 races knowing that a McLaren would win barring some sort of unnatural disaster; but the key was that you never knew whether it would be Ayrton Senna or Alain Prost who took the chequered flag first. That added a wonderful frisson of excitement to each encounter. Ferrari's technical domination was no different in 2002, but always, it seemed, it had to be Schumacher who won and there is never a story in predictability. On the occasions when Barrichello had him beaten, such as Austria, the Brazilian was obliged to concede victory; on the occasions when he was 'allowed' to win, after Ferrari got its knuckles rapped by the FIA and team orders were supposedly outlawed, it was so obvious that games were being played that it merely added to the hapless Brazilian's embarrassment.

'Serves him right,' his critics said. 'He took the big money at Ferrari. Nobody forced him to. What else did he expect with Schumacher?'

Barrichello himself maintained a dignified silence. Materially, yes, he had made himself a wealthy man and safeguarded his family's future. It's any man's right to maximise his income. And as a driver he had made yet more progress. He had shown the potential to emerge from the awesome shadow of Schumacher, and the fighting spirit to do so. And he was fast without making mistakes. The fact that Ferrari at times had to slow him down was tacit acknowledgement of that. But what he really felt about being forced to play second fiddle he kept to himself, hidden behind an unhappy mask. In public he played the game that Ferrari imposed upon him, only rarely letting his guard down, while privately focusing his determination on beating Schumacher in 2003. His plan was to do so on sheer merit, so that they *had* to let him win.

Chapter 11

SO NEAR YET
SO FAR, 2003

Rubens Barrichello began 2003 with very high goals. 'Last year,' he said, 'I felt I drove the best I have ever done in Formula One, but I had bad luck at the start of the season. Now I am older, happier, and faster. I am hoping to make a better start this time and I am looking for the title, even though some people might say it is impossible with Michael as my teammate.

'But it is very close between us, as we have seen in recent testing. I have improved a lot since I came to Ferrari, and part of that is because of Michael. But it is not a case of copying him, as everyone has to solve their own problems and there is no sign that he is getting slower.'

Besides the inevitable challenge of his teammate, Barrichello joined all the other drivers and teams in contending with completely new regulations.

First, drivers now had to start a race with the fuel that was left over from their qualifying run. This, instead of comprising four runs in one hour, had been cut to a single lap, which really meant one run comprising an out lap, a timed flying lap, and an in lap. What this meant was that qualifying was no longer a reflection of out-and-out pace, but instead became clouded by the secrecy of a team's refuelling strategy. You could, for example, run a light fuel load that would only get you through, say, 15 laps of the race, before you needed to refuel. That would get you near the front of the grid, but it might not be the ideal policy for a race. Or you might elect to run 25 laps before refuelling. You might go for two refuelling stops in a race, or just one. In extremis, maybe even three. Strategy thus became of paramount importance, and to begin with all sorts of ploys would be tried. Renault in particular, and Ferrari to an extent, would become the authors of sound strategic plans, but before long everyone cottoned on and began to follow similar gameplans.

Then there was the requirement that a driver could only use one engine for the entire Grand Prix weekend. If you suffered a failure and needed a new engine (in either practice or qualifying), you lost ten grid places.

On top of all that, the points scoring system had also been changed. You still got ten points for a win, but now it was worth only two points more than second place, not four, as the points-scoring positions were extended down to eighth place. So, instead of 10-6-4-3-2-1, the system was now 10-8-6-5-4-3-2-1.

The overall effect was to make it much harder for a driver to be totally consistent during the season, and in many ways the regulations created one of the most exciting seasons for years as no fewer than eight different drivers won races. You had to go back to 1983 and 1985 for similar results. While this injected some desperately needed fresh lifeblood into a sport that was in danger of murdering its self-created golden goose after the year of Ferrari domination in 2002, it was not great news for Barrichello. Ferrari president Luca di Montezemolo was taking the broad view of the sport, and not speaking specifically of the tough time that Ferrari sometimes experienced, when he said: '2003 was a very difficult year, very stressing.' But in some ways that was a concise summary of how the Brazilian felt.

Once again Ferrari began the new season with an updated version of its old car, and this time when the new car appeared – in Spain in May – both drivers got it at the same time.

Australia saw both relying on the trusty F2002, but a shock awaited Ferrari as Kimi Räikkönen drove a feisty race in which he clashed with Michael after refusing to give ground. That delayed both of them and allowed David Coulthard to take the first win of the season in the sister McLaren. Schumacher, who had started from pole, wound up fourth, but for Barrichello Melbourne marked another non-finish. He started second to Schumacher and ran behind him in second place until crashing after a brief rain shower. It was not an auspicious start, and already there was a suspicion that in greasy conditions Bridgestone's tyre lacked the performance of Michelin's.

In Malaysia Schumacher was delayed after a first corner clash with Jarno Trulli's Renault, and though he set fastest lap he could only finish sixth. Barrichello had a much better race, finishing second albeit well beaten by Räikkönen.

He went to Brazil full of great hopes, and promptly qualified on pole position in front of his adoring fans. Heavy rain was a characteristic of this race, and saw Michael make the sort of mistake that Rubens assiduously avoided while running right behind him. As the German crashed on a river in Turn Three, Barrichello led the first eight laps behind the safety car (so bad were the conditions) then dropped momentarily behind Michelin runner Coulthard before the similarly shod Räikkönen and Montoya also muscled past a lap later. Mark Webber in a Jaguar (on Michelins) and Schumacher also deposed him, but he was content to bide his time in the dire conditions. Schumacher crashed out on the 27th lap, and, as Räikkönen refuelled, Barrichello – who had stopped earlier – moved into second place behind Coulthard on lap 28. The Scot had refuelled at the same time (lap 19), and now they engaged in a battle for the lead. After dogging the McLaren, Rubens finally pulled off his move on the 45th lap, to the delight of his bedraggled countrymen. Two laps later, however, just as it seemed that everything was finally going to work out for the hometown hero, their cries of delight turned to groans of despair as the red car faltered and then rolled to a silent halt. Initially Ferrari suggested that he had been the victim of electronic problems, but gradually it began to filter out that he had run out of fuel. It seemed unthinkable for the world's best team, but there it was.

Much later in the year, when the wound had healed, spokesman Luca Colajanni explained: 'The rain had interfered with the telemetry so we had no clear idea of his fuel consumption, that's why he ran out.'

It was no consolation to Barrichello that he also set fastest lap.

Schumacher was back in the hunt at Imola, where he started from pole, set fastest lap, and won, and Barrichello was back in the points in third place, the pair separated by Räikkönen, who was already shaping up as Schumacher's main rival for the title. The Finn had 32 points as he left Italy, to Coulthard's 19 and Schumacher's 18. Barrichello was fifth with 14, behind the impressive Spaniard Fernando Alonso who was teamed with Trulli at Renault.

The Spanish Grand Prix in Barcelona marked the debut of the new Ferrari F2003, which had the suffix GA added after the death in January of Fiat scion Gianni Agnelli. The car had been waiting in the wings all season, but first the team needed to improve its reliability – there had been some heavy shunts because of at least two suspension breakages in testing. Now it was deemed almost bullet-proof, and Schumacher won with it straight out of the box, from pole, and Barrichello brought his home third with fastest lap. It nearly ended in tears, however, as Schumacher pulled one of his trademark close moves to snatch the lead from Barrichello in the first corner. It looked pretty ruthless, but Barrichello seemed quite calm about it afterwards regardless of what he might have thought at the time.

'I don't think I've ever been so close to Michael!' he admitted. 'I think we were closer than this, probably,' he added, indicating a tiny gap between finger and thumb. 'But it was a good first corner actually, because I had to try to overtake Fernando and I saw that Michael chose the inside line to protect his line so I was braking on the right tarmac and I just said I'll give it a go. I did actually go through a little bit in front but we were too close. I had to give way a little bit and then I went on the grass, so therefore I couldn't keep the line. But that shows how much we respect each other and how much we have fun together.'

Australia 2000: Barrichello's debut for Ferrari could scarcely have gone better, a strong drive netting him second place to team leader Michael Schumacher, and fastest lap.

On Ferrari's home ground at Imola, Barrichello brought his F2000 home fourth.

Left: *Bearded Barrichello: for a while, a new team meant a new look.*

Below: *Silverstone 2000 gave Barrichello his best chance to show the form he had with Stewart in 1999, as he led from pole position until hydraulic problems intervened.*

Right: *Monte Carlo 2000 proved a re-run of the 1997 result, with Barrichello chasing home Schumacher.*

Left: *Another podium result, this time third place at Magny-Cours.*

Below left: *Finally the big day arrived at Hockenheim, on 30 July 2000. A superb drive in the wet yielded Barrichello his maiden grand prix triumph.*

Right: *Mobil's advertising number in the background is apposite as Barrichello, his tears drying, begins to savour his breakthrough achievement.*

Below: *2001 brought Barrichello a repeat of his 1999 disappointment at home in Interlagos, where he led …*

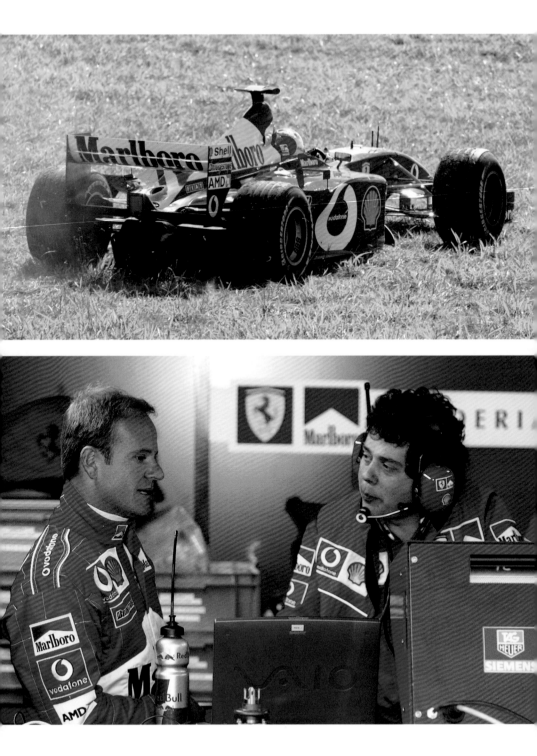

Above left: ... *until his Ferrari succumbed to mechanical woes.*

Left: *During the 2001 season, Barrichello worked strongly with his race engineer, former Sauber employee Gabriele Dellacolli.*

Above: *In Austria the true meaning of life at Ferrari became clear to Barrichello when he was instructed to let teammate Michael Schumacher through, for what should have been his own second victory.*

Right: *His face taut, a bitterly disappointed Barrichello faced the media with dignity after the official press conference.*

Things were back on an even keel by Hungary, however, where Barrichello celebrated another one–two on the podium with Jean Todt and Schumacher.

Austria in 2002 brought a terrible sense of déjà vu as Barrichello was yet again told to let Schumacher win.

As Schumacher pushed Barrichello on to the top step of the podium in Austria, their body language reeked of awkwardness and embarrassment.

With the threat of FIA censure hanging over Ferrari's head, there could be no team orders at the 2002 Nürburgring. In parc ferme Schumacher congratulates Barrichello on his victory.

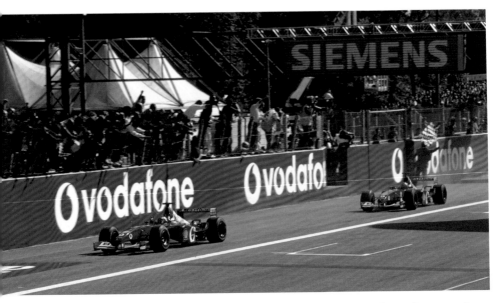

A fortnight later he was the one on the top step, after leading Schumacher across the line at Monza.

Indianapolis 2002: the crowd booed when Schumacher gifted Barrichello another victory, as his attempt to stage a dead heat over the famed line of bricks backfired.

In Japan, their success went to Barrichello and Schumacher's heads …

Barrichello celebrates victory in November 2002's Granja Viana 500, with teammates Tony Kanaan and Felipe Massa.

Left: *Barrichello savours his greatest triumph to date as he waves to the crowds during the slowing down lap at Silverstone in July 2003.*

Below left: *Japan yielded Barrichello another excellent win, from pole position. He led initially from Alonso and Montoya, and his victory helped to ensure teammate Schumacher's sixth championship crown.*

Right: *The delight is evident in every aspect of Barrichello's demeanour as he hoists the Japanese trophy aloft …*

Below: *… while later on he, Ross Brawn, Jean Todt, and Schumacher look a little the worse for wear as they celebrate into the night at Suzuka.*

When you win for Ferrari there is no place better to do it than the great team's home ground at Monza. As the tifosi go mad at the 2004 event, Barrichello savours one of his greatest moments.

No sooner had the tumult and shouting of Monza subsided than Barrichello, seen here leading Kimi Räikkönen, sped home to another victory for Ferrari as the Formula One circus visited China for the first time.

The pressure is always high for Rubens in Brazil, where his fans turn out in their thousands to cheer him on.

In January 2005, before the start of yet another world championship campaign, there was time for fun racing karts on ice with Schumacher at a Ferrari press event at Madonna Campiglio.

Among his talents as an athlete, Barrichello counts his prowess on a snowboard.

The passion is never far from the surface and when Barrichello speaks publicly he does so with style and candour, frequently with his heart on his sleeve.

Cynics were unconvinced, especially as the move cost him second place to the fleet Alonso.

Even Schumacher wasn't sure whether they had actually touched. 'He thinks no, I don't actually know,' he said, referring to Barrichello, 'but it was very close because he quite rightly pulled in because he was slightly in front after he braked very late and I didn't expect him there. I was still there so I had to go over the inside kerb a little bit on the dirt. I slid then and I thought, during the slide, that I was going into him, but I think he slid at the same time. We just would have had a light touch, but that's the way it has to be. It's racing and it's competition.'

A relieved Ross Brawn felt the F2003-GA was a major step forward over the F2002, and rated its potential much higher. 'We'd plateaud out with the old car on the engine, chassis, and everything, and with this new car there are things to do on the chassis and things to do on the engine. We are just starting,' he said.

The Ferrari drivers repeated the result in Austria, but with Räikkönen separating them on the podium the scores were now Räikkönen 40 points, Schumacher 38, Barrichello 26.

The Monaco Grand Prix marked the emergence of the BMW Williams drivers as potential title contenders, as Juan Pablo Montoya won from Räikkönen and Ralf Schumacher chased his brother home in fourth place. But for Barrichello it was an afternoon very much to forget as he could only manage eighth place.

Canada was little better, although he did finish fifth as Michael squeezed out a clever win over brother Ralf even though he was in brake trouble. The younger Schumacher was roundly criticised for failing to mount a convincing attack on his elder sibling. This was a crucial result for the champion, as it now gave him the title lead over Räikkönen by three points.

It was Schumacher's turn for fifth at the Nürburgring, but Barrichello felt happier after taking the final podium slot behind the BMW Williams duo after early leader Räikkönen had departed with a blown engine that, in retrospect, arguably cost him that year's title. At the start Barrichello was actually ahead of Montoya, but a later spell with poor handling balance cost him pace.

Ralf Schumacher and Juan Pablo Montoya repeated the German result in the heat of Magny-Cours during the French Grand Prix, where Schumacher drove brilliantly to take a third place that should have been beyond his reach as Michelin again crushed Bridgestone. Barrichello was in the points again, but only scored two for a lowly seventh place after starting eighth. He desperately needed to raise his game, and the British Grand Prix on the dauntingly quick Silverstone track finally provided him with the means to do just that.

'Up until Silverstone it had been difficult to start with,' he admitted, 'and when I got there I was criticised for everything else. I spun in Friday's qualifying, but the big thing about myself is that nowadays I am more critical of myself and I don't really care what other people say. I have to be organised within myself and just be happy. And if I am not happy it's because I am not doing well, and something needs to be sorted out. What I learned then was that I was trying something different that didn't work, so on Saturday morning I went a different route.'

Just as the criticism of him was reaching a crescendo, support came in the avuncular form of Ross Brawn.

'It has just been a few unfortunate circumstances,' he said, 'and there is a fine line between success and failure in this business as we have seen from last year to this year with our team. There are far more people capable of filling the top six positions in the race, so if you make a little mistake at the moment then you lose it. Last year, Rubens started this race in pole position and came second. You can't do that at the moment and if you have a glitch or a problem then you are out of the running. He has had a few little unfortunate events. What often happens is it seems to fall to one driver in a team and it looks very odd but I think all the things that have happened … his qualifying at the last race, there was an adjustment made between warm-up and qualifying that was not correct and that caught him out in qualifying. So then he started a bit further back than he should have been and his race became very difficult.

'There is a very fine line at the moment and it is a more normal year in that respect. Rubens is a very good driver and he is obviously being compared to Michael, who is exceptional, exceptional for the last several generations, so he has a tough job in that respect. But we are happy with Rubens's performance and if we get our package more competitive then Rubens would be doing a similar job to what he did last year.'

Barrichello clearly had things sorted out after his spin on Friday, in the qualifying session that would determine the starting order for Saturday's hour of qualifying. He was expected to struggle on then, but instead he rose magnificently to the challenge to plant his F2003-GA firmly on pole.

To an extent, history repeated itself in one of the best races of the season.

Barrichello was beaten off the line by Jarno Trulli, whose Renault had great traction control software. The Italian led for five laps until deployment of the safety car bunched the field on lap six while debris – the headrest from David Coulthard's McLaren – was cleared away from Copse corner. When racing resumed on lap eight Trulli rebuilt his lead, chased by Räikkönen and Barrichello. But on lap 12 a stupid spectator making an apparently religious protest (he carried a banner with the words 'Read the Bible, the Bible is always right') began running down Hangar Straight – the fastest part of the course – into the path of the cars exiting Chapel Curve. The safety car was immediately redeployed, and stayed out until lap 15 as former priest Neil Horan, a religious activist, was rugby tackled by a marshal and hauled away for psychiatric reports.

This prompted a rash of pit stops on the 12th lap: in came Trulli, Barrichello (who had sneaked by Räikkönen at Abbey Curve), Räikkönen, Ralf Schumacher, Michael Schumacher,

Montoya, Fernando Alonso, Jacques Villeneuve, Mark Webber, Nick Heidfeld, and Jenson Button. Inevitably, the second cars in each team lost time as they waited for their teammates to be serviced. Particularly affected by this were Alonso and Schumacher Snr, though both Montoya and the Spaniard slipped ahead of the world champion in the pit stop process.

As things settled down Räikkönen led, chased by Barrichello, who had tigered through the traffic after a big fight with Trulli and Coulthard. Behind him, Montoya was looking strong as Alonso moved up to chase Trulli. But for Schumacher it was a nightmare for many laps as he sat in 13th place, trapped behind the crocodile of Firman, Webber, Pizzonia, Villeneuve, and Alonso. The Spaniard and the French-Canadian proved particularly resistant to his attempts to pass, and at this stage the amount of time he lost would seal his fate.

When Räikkönen pitted on lap 35 Barrichello went into the lead for the first time, chased by Montoya and the Renaults. Räikkönen went back ahead when the Ferrari was refuelled on lap 39, but it was immediately obvious that the red car was faster than the silver one. Räikkönen stayed ahead on laps 40 and 41, but on lap 42, while fending off pressure from Barrichello at Bridge corner, the McLaren slid wide. Barrichello pounced immediately, and moved into a lead he would not subsequently surrender.

The last time that a lunatic spectator had invaded a race track during a Grand Prix was at Hockenheim three years earlier, and on that occasion the winner was also R. Barrichello. 'I don't condone the behaviour,' he beamed, 'But clearly there must be something in it for me! I was really confident of our new tyres and I knew I had a car that was fast enough for me to pull away.

'When I overtook Kimi I was being careful because, to be honest, it was with a McLaren some time ago that I crashed into Abbey. I was paying attention because the guy who has the inside protecting the line can brake a lot earlier than you think, so I pulled away to the right at the right moment, but I almost lost my nose at that time. It was fair, but it was aggressive. We went into bridge like it was one coming out. But it was fair, it was good.'

It was a brilliant triumph, made all the sweeter as it vindicated him after all the criticism he'd had to endure in 2003. Fastest lap was the icing on the cake after the most convincing and commanding performance of Barrichello's Formula One career.

'I love to be inside a team where they work like they worked last week to make this car better and like Bridgestone work to make the tyres better. But the last two weeks people have been saying so many things about the first-lap crashing Rubens, this and that, so I hope they shut up now. I overtook a lot of people.'

Altogether, the 2003 British Grand Prix was a fantastic race, with more overtaking in this one event than in all the other 2003 races put together. But not if you were Schumacher, who appeared to drive what by his lofty standards was a somewhat feeble race. Eventually he finished fourth, but it was fair to say that this was one of those rare races in which he never really featured. It was a point that was not lost on Barrichello.

'In the end I won Silverstone in a fantastic way, overtaking and so on, and it was marvellous. But then I had a little bit of an unlucky time after that.'

The bad luck started again in Germany, where Michael finished only seventh after a race full of dramas, and Rubens failed to finish after being eliminated in a start-line shunt with Räikkönen when he was squeezed by Ralf Schumacher and inadvertently collected the fast-starting Finn's McLaren. Eventually the drivers were called to a tribunal, where the incident was rightly written off as a racing accident.

'I had just started in Hockenheim and there was no aggression because you just had to go forward,' he related. 'All of a sudden there was a crash. I don't think we were actually trying to fight. We didn't know we were so close.'

The most annoying aspect for him was that he had chosen different Bridgestones to Schumacher's and believed he had made the right decision. 'I felt comfortable with the tyres for the whole weekend, not enough to beat the BMW Williams in qualifying but my tyres should have worked quite well in the heat on Sunday...'

There was similar disappointment in Hungary, too, where Ferrari – read Bridgestone – was well beaten. Michael was a weak eighth in his least convincing drive to date, beaten by seven Michelin runners in the order Alonso, Räikkönen, Montoya, Ralf Schumacher, Coulthard, Webber, and Trulli. Barrichello went out after 19 laps when, heading for the first corner, the entire left-hand rear suspension parted company with his car after a mechanical failure. Most likely a driveshaft sheared at the inboard end and, flailing around, destroyed the suspension. The Ferrari was immediately pitched into a lurid spin into the lengthy gravel trap, the only consolation being that it was probably the most opportune place on the circuit for such a thing to happen, and only a relatively short walk back to the pits.

There was an air of crisis within the Ferrari camp now. The F2003-GA was certainly a better car than the dominant F2002, and it was clear that Bridgestone was being hammered by Michelin. But though Hungary looked like the nadir when Schumacher could only finish eighth, Bridgestone's senior development engineer Kees van der Grint was adamant that their two worst races were Magny-Cours and Hockenheim. It was easy to forget that Barrichello was fighting for second place initially at the Hungaroring, or even that Schumacher was running second (albeit a very distant second) to Montoya at Hockenheim before he sustained a puncture that dropped him to seventh.

After Hungary Ferrari and Bridgestone approached the FIA, protesting that Michelin's front tyre tread width, though legal when measured new, was 5mm over the 270mm limit when worn. Under the rules the tyres were measured when new. But now the FIA 'reinterpreted' its own ruling to measure the tyres when worn, and agreed with Ferrari and Bridgestone. Harsh words were exchanged all round, and as Michelin threatened to sue Ross Brawn for inflammatory remarks he had allegedly made on tape to a journalist, Ferrari threatened to protest some 2003 results retrospectively. Suddenly a great season was thrown into confusion as Michelin had to modify its moulds between Hungary and Monza to make some revised tyres. This led to the most acrimonious press conference in years at Monza, where Brawn came under fire from Patrick Head, the technical director of BMW Williams, and McLaren team principal Ron Dennis. The latter, speaking of the disruption that had been caused, said: 'From my youth I remember seeing a film, *Ben Hur*, and one sequence where the slaves are flogged to row at what was called "ramming speed", the maximum speed for hitting rivals. And ramming speed is what a grand prix team achieves at the point at which a world championship becomes as critical and finely balanced as it is now. This definitely had a negative influence and I think that was part of the strategy.'

The net effect of the acrimonious controversy was that Bridgestone and Ferrari picked themselves up. Whether this was the result of sheer hard work from both parties, or of the after-effect of the protest which undoubtedly destabilised the efforts of the two principal rivals, Williams and McLaren, at crucial times in their campaigns, was a matter of personal opinion and that varied greatly in the paddock. Some argued that a championship won by a Michelin driver would be tainted after the accusations; others that a championship won by Bridgestone-shod Michael Schumacher would be equally tainted because of them. Whatever your view, it would prove to be the turning point of the season.

Now the Ferraris were back on the pace, and Schumacher won the Italian Grand Prix comfortably from Montoya's BMW Williams, with Barrichello third, hard on the Colombian's heels and with Räikkönen in turn hounding his Ferrari as his rear tyres went off.

Schumacher also won the US Grand Prix at Indianapolis as changeable weather conditions mid-race played into his hands and frustrated early walkaway leader Räikkönen, who had to settle for second. While they faced off for the finale at Suzuka, with Michael having all the advantage with 92 points to the Finn's 83 (thereby giving Räikkönen only an outside chance of winning overall if he won the race and Schumacher failed to score any points), Barrichello headed for Japan determined to set things right. His US Grand Prix was little short of a disaster. Having qualified on the front row alongside polesitter Räikkönen, he had responded with a big grin to the question of what role he intended to play on race day with the quip: 'Hopefully to win the race, I think that's the first plan right now.'

Instead, he found himself attacked in the early going by a perhaps over-optimistic Montoya on the third lap as the Colombian sought to keep his own championship aspirations alive. Montoya was duly punished (harshly, some thought) by a stop-and-go penalty that killed his title hopes, but Barrichello was spun into immediate retirement. He'd lost time when second gear baulked thanks to a faulty automatic upshift at the start, and found himself running side-by-side with Montoya. 'I thought I had left him enough space, but he touched me and I spun...'

Räikkönen needed to win the Japanese Grand Prix with Schumacher ninth or worse. It was a tall order, but when rain intervened as Michael, brother Ralf, and Jarno Trulli did their qualifying laps, hopes sprang up chez McLaren and dived at Ferrari. If Schumacher has a weakness, it is while fighting in the pack, and as the champion struggled to seventh on the grid while Barrichello took the pole with Montoya alongside him, one Ferrari insider murmured: 'Shit! Now we're in for a bloody awful race if Michael is that far back.'

These things are relative, however. It was indeed a poor race for Schumacher. Spectacularly poor, actually, as he drove like a novice rather than a multiple world champion. He barely featured in a race notable more for the errors he made. Chasing Takuma Sato for 12th place on the sixth lap he damaged his front wing crashing into the back of the Japanese driver's BAR Honda at the chicane, dropping to last place.

On lap 41 he got his braking wrong again there, locked up to avoid hitting Cristiano da Matta's Toyota, and pulled into the path of brother Ralf, who couldn't avoid hitting his left rear tyre. Both Schumachers slid down the escape road, and subsequently Michael admitted to worries about a puncture for the rest of his race to an undistinguished eighth place finish that was all he needed to take the championship.

But it was anything but a poor race for Ferrari, thanks to a superb performance by Barrichello which matched his race at Silverstone for style and effectiveness. Montoya put in a blistering initial performance, snatching the lead and pulling away until Barrichello stabilised the gap and then began closing it. But then the Brazilian caught a break as the Colombian dropped out on the tenth lap with a hydraulic problem. Apart from in the immediate aftermath of his three pit stops, he held the lead to the finish, comfortably outpacing Räikkönen and Coulthard. And as long as he sat there, it didn't matter what sort of a hash Michael was making further back. So long as Barrichello prevented Räikkönen from winning, what Michael himself did was academic.

It was, however, an edgy race. At various points any slip from Barrichello could have gifted the title to Räikkönen, but in the end the result worked out the way most had predicted. Michael Schumacher won his record sixth world championship crown, and Ferrari wrapped up the constructors' title, as Barrichello won by 11 seconds. His performance not only illustrated what he can do on his day, but also underlined his value as the team player par excellence. Whatever Ferrari was paying him, it was money well spent on days such as that.

'I'm so proud to be have helped Ferrari win four of their five recent titles and to win this race on what is considered a drivers' circuit is another reason to be proud,' the delighted Brazilian gasped. 'Along with Silverstone this year, these are the two best races of my life. I want to thank everyone at home in Brazil for staying up to watch and this victory pays them back.

'You cannot compare drivers from different generations, but what Michael has done today is a fantastic achievement.'

Clearly affected by his own success, which brought down the curtain on a great season of Formula One that was as exciting as 2002 had been predictable, Schumacher said: 'It's probably not appropriate to describe my emotions. It's been a tough year and tough late stage of season, and this was a very tough race, probably one of my toughest. But much more to mention is the team. They did an incredible job, Rubens had a fantastic drive winning in great style, so we won the constructors' title now five times in a row, the first time this has ever happened, and we did it in big style. You have seen what happened in Nürburgring, Hockenheim, and Budapest, and how many people wrote us off. But here we are, back, because we never give up, we always fight. That's one of the strengths of a fantastic team.'

The seventh victory of Barrichello's career pushed him to fourth overall on 65 points, separated from Michael by Räikkönen and Montoya.

'After Silverstone I felt brilliant,' he revealed later. 'I went to Germany feeling on top of the world, and I think I could have done really well at Hockenheim. I didn't win, but it was going to be close with Montoya. I had different tyres to Michael. Then in Hungary I could have finished on the podium and instead I finished in the wall, so I could have had many more points, maybe even fought for the championship. But the finale was fantastic. Japan for me has always been a place where I wanted to do well, one of the most challenging places. And I put it on pole, even though I was a little bit lucky that the rain gave Michael, Ralf, and Trulli problems with drizzle. I had a very, very good time and I won, so I finished the season on a real high. I think I have had a much better year in terms of my performance, compared to last year when I had more points and was higher in the championship.'

Japan and Silverstone were precisely the kind of performances he had dreamed of when he first came into Formula One back in

1993. 'And Silverstone has been my home anyway with all the racing and testing I had done there, so that race meant a lot to me. It was nice to have won there in F3, and now in F1. I would say Silverstone, Japan, and Brazil, and Spa – those are the races where I told myself I had to win.'

Two down, two to go.

So the season ultimately yielded Schumacher his record sixth world championship crown. But various aspects of his year raised questions about him. The shunt in the rain in Brazil, the tangle with Montoya in Germany, the way it took him so long to pass Alonso at Silverstone (where he eventually shoved the Renault driver to one side), and the feeble performance in Suzuka. Was it really time for the remarkable German to consider hanging up his helmet? Were the first signs beginning to show that he was past his best? Was it time – whisper it – for Ferrari to let Barrichello have his turn as team leader?

While some people wondered about Schumacher, on the ridiculous age-old basis that a driver – even one as great as he was – is only as good as his last race, that same basis for comparison showed Barrichello in a better light than ever. Taken in tandem with his result at Silverstone, his great victory at Suzuka elevated him to a position to which he had long aspired yet had never quite been able to lay claim. Like astronaut Gordo Cooper, Rubinho had gone higher, further, and faster than anyone else, and it did not go unnoticed that his great drive had been instrumental in aiding Schumacher's cause when help was most needed.

Despite all that there were whispers that Ferrari might try to grab Kimi Räikkönen from McLaren, or Fernando Alonso from Renault, contracts notwithstanding, and they weren't going to be replacements for Michael Schumacher. There was talk of Barrichello moving elsewhere of his own volition, too. But at the end of the season it was clear he would be staying put, and he got a big vote of confidence within Ferrari.

'He did a wonderful job in 2003 – he has matured each year and looked especially good when you think how he was when he came to us in 2000,' press relations manager Luca Colajanni suggested. 'To choose the right tyre and to get the car set up so well – that is the glory of the driver!'

Technical director Ross Brawn thought he had always been underrated. 'He has always been a valued member of the team. He and Michael share all of their information and many times Michael has taken Rubens's set-up, and vice versa. The single lap qualifying has affected the way we run practice and prequalifying, and the drivers often have different paths so we can choose which is better. Rubens has contributed even more in 2003 and we have always been totally confident in all that he has done. He always contributes to a high level. In 2003 Kimi Räikkönen, Fernando Alonso, and Juan Pablo Montoya were all tough competition for Michael, but Rubens kept him very sharp.'

Brawn was always adamant that what he least wanted on the F2003-GA was an operational sweet spot, because he wanted a car that could perform equally strongly in a wide range of operating conditions and set-ups. But over the course of the season, especially in the middle, that was what it often had. It was why Barrichello often outqualified Schumacher, for the Brazilian used his set-up talents to find the sweet spot and sometimes the German didn't quite. A tiny degree made a big difference, which could hurt the lap times.

Sporting director Jean Todt reminded the world that even Schumacher had been off the road 20 times during the course of a very hard year – 'Even with that it didn't embarrass him as he won the world championship' – but he was laudatory about Barrichello, and added: 'We are very happy with him. He has impressed a lot, and we don't see any particular reasons not to move forward as we are.'

Now all Barrichello had to do was put together a seasonful of races such as Silverstone and Suzuka, against the greatest driver of his era. He went into 2004 confident that he might, at last, be just able to do that.

There was good reason to believe that was possible, even if Schumacher had made it clear he was far from ready to consider retirement. 'Our main fear this year was complacency,' Ross Brawn said, 'if we got a little soft. Last year was, after all, pretty good for us. But this year our car was not optimised. Nobody's was because the regulations were so late coming, but it was a question of degree. 2003 certainly woke us up for the winter, to make us as competitive as possible for the new season.'

Ferrari, however, was hardly in the doldrums, as the team celebrated its fifth successive world constructors' title and had won the last race. 2003 might not have been Rubens Barrichello's greatest season (though it did yield his two best victories), but he could take heart that he was driving for the best team with the most cohesive band of engineers and was himself doing a great job in the cockpit most of the time. And he could look forward to a much stronger effort in 2004 after the scare Ferrari had had.

'I always say this in our "secret of success" lecture,' Ferrari's chief designer Rory Byrne said: 'You always have to consider change; if you stand still, you go backwards. Michelin was a strong competitor in 2003, but there were a lot of new initiatives from Bridgestone and we were encouraged that, like us, Bridgestone recognised the need to intensify their efforts. Next year we will be much stronger.'

There was every reason for him to hope that 2004 might finally be The Year.

Chapter 12

BETTER THAN
EVER, 2004

It was that shrewdest of Formula One observers, Sir Frank Williams, who was the only man to admit openly that Ferrari's F2003-GA was still the best car of the 2003 season, despite being let down by the occasional poor performance of its Bridgestone tyres in comparison with its Michelin-shod rivals. Many people were sceptical when he made the comment, for self-delusion is just as much a part of Formula One as camber angles and gear ratios. But 2004 would prove him absolutely right. Running on significantly better Bridgestones developed over the winter by Kees van der Grint and his team in Japan, and itself an improved version of its forerunner, Ferrari's F2004 put the red team back in a class of its own.

Predictably, Michael Schumacher won a record seventh world championship title, having at one stage seemed frighteningly likely to win every single race, while Ferrari clinched an unprecedented sixth consecutive constructors' championship thanks to its drivers' tally of 262 points. Off the track things behind the scenes reached a level of acrimony and uncertainty unseen since the FISA/FOCA war of 1980 and would result in the Scuderia being isolated from its rivals by the end of the season, but on the track, despite winning 15 of the 18 races, Ferrari did have some opposition as Renault, McLaren, and BMW Williams each won a race. But the strongest overall opponent proved to be BAR Honda, even though neither Jenson Button nor Takuma Sato quite managed a win.

Right from the start the Ferraris demonstrated an advantage of 0.7s a lap, and for the most part it remained that way all through.

By Monza they were actually 1.3s quicker than the next best challenger, Antonio Pizzonia's BMW Williams.

Straight out of the box Schumacher won the opening five races. He started from pole position in Australia, Malaysia, and Bahrain, which had joined the grand prix circus for the first time. In the first and second races he also set fastest lap. He won in Imola with fastest lap in front of the adoring *tifosi*, who had been stunned when Jenson Button beat the red cars to pole position in qualifying, and he recorded another clean sweep in Spain.

By then, Ferrari's opposition and its fans had long since given up any hope that the Italian team would have to fight all the way to the Brazilian Grand Prix, which would end the 18-race series at Interlagos in October.

But where was Rubens Barrichello in all this?

Having so dominated Suzuka the previous season, he had impressed some people enough for them to demand that he got equal billing with Schumacher, whose weak performance there had triggered suggestions that perhaps he was tiptoeing past his prime. Clearly, as his opening 2004 salvo proved all too conclusively, this was not the case. For Barrichello, his resurgence would prove demoralising, especially since it coincided with yet another streak of ill fortune.

He opened his year finishing second to Michael in Albert Park, only 1.37 seconds behind, but Malaysia yielded only fourth place as Juan Pablo Montoya and Button edged between his Ferrari and Schumacher's. His tyre choice proved less beneficial than Michael's and he was a little concerned about brake efficiency. He was also unhappy to lose the time while lapping Minardi driver Zsolt Baumgartner that would later equate to the deficit to Button in third place.

On Bahrain's dry and dusty new Sakhir circuit he looked likely to snatch the lead from Schumacher at the start after making a better start from the front row of the grid, but at the very last moment Michael outbraked him and shouldered into a lead he never looked like surrendering. To some that was a telling moment. 'It's easy to do things like that when you know you have a teammate who will ultimately yield to you,' one cynic was heard to remark.

'I almost had to avoid Michael,' Barrichello said, 'and then he was very, very fast for the first couple of corners, so he got a gap.'

Second place in the desert was followed by only sixth in Imola, as Button and Montoya were joined by the Renaults of Fernando Alonso and Jarno Trulli in the top five places behind Schumacher.

The Ferraris were first and second again in Spain, where Barrichello trailed Schumacher by just over 13 seconds after choosing a two-stop strategy in contrast to Schumacher's three which enabled the latter to run a lighter car. Even when Michael tripped up and committed a faux pas in the tunnel at Monaco which denied him the chance of six in a row, Barrichello was not there to pick up the pieces after starting only seventh. 'I think I was very lucky to finish today, and third place was my present from God,' he said afterwards. On that occasion the win went to Trulli, with Button right on his gearbox, and the best the Brazilian could do was third, a long way off their pace having struggled all afternoon with a car that was so wayward, and bottomed so often, that he was convinced something in the suspension had been damaged.

Schumacher quickly picked up after his kerfuffle with Montoya at Monaco which had put him out of the race, winning the next seven events – Europe, Canada, US, France, Britain, Germany, and Hungary. He did it with such majesty that not even Barrichello, who had so trounced him at Suzuka, got a look in. It was wonderful for Ferrari, a nightmare for everyone else. But nobody could fairly blame a team for doing such a superb job. It was, after all, what it was there to do. Ferrari was operating once again with such complete synergy that it utterly redefined the word 'teamwork'.

While Michael was on top of the world again, his former teammate Eddie Irvine took time out from retirement to launch a broadside at his replacement. In his column in *The Sun* newspaper, he said: 'If Rubens Barrichello uses tomorrow's European Grand Prix to give another string of excuses as to why he didn't win, someone should give him a slap. I'm fed up with hearing Ferrari's number two whinge every time he is outdriven by Michael Schumacher. It grates on me having to listen to him moan his brakes weren't working properly, his second set of tyres were off or the balance of his car was never perfect. There's always a problem and I'm sick and tired of seeing his long face after he cruised around for a few safe points.'

There was a lot more in that vein, as Barrichello's former Jordan partner unloaded himself while apparently forgetting some of his own post-race comments when he had been the Ferrari driver being whipped by Michael.

Once again running a two-stop strategy to Schumacher's three, Barrichello duly followed him home again at the Nürburgring, where he reflected on his tough start to a year which had seemed to hold such promise for him.

Why hadn't things gelled for him the way they had for Michael?

'I was really quick in qualifying in Australia, within a hundredth of Michael and I had a really good race, pushing him to the limit,' he began. 'Then after that I'd do something that didn't work as well. I'd choose a tyre, choose a different brake for the rain, things I hoped might give me an edge over him. Sometimes I didn't qualify as well as a result, so whenever I had a car that was stronger than his in race trim, he was already seven seconds in front. I would be stuck in the traffic the whole race, like I was at Imola. Barcelona didn't go according to my plans. In Monaco again it was a bad qualifying for us both – he was fourth and I was only sixth – and I had an eventful race. We found something very small upset us in qualifying and the car wouldn't do the things that I wanted, so the only thing I would say was the tyre. The car felt really strange in the second stint, on the second set of tyres.'

The fact that Schumacher was getting the best from the car when he was not, in direct contrast to previous seasons, led to suggestions in the paddock that his performances in Silverstone and Suzuka the previous year had so worried Schumacher that he had instructed Ferrari that Barrichello was no longer allowed to be privy to his set-up. At the time of our interview a representative from Ferrari was sitting in (such is the trusting way of Formula One in the 21st century), but as he answered Barrichello did not appear to be dissembling.

'No, that's not true at all. I have full access to his and he has full access to mine. Sometimes he takes my set-up, but sometimes I take his. That happens a lot between us. Last year it happened a lot with Michael. I'm not trying to find an excuse, because I have to keep my head working and my foot down and try to make it work, but eventually you have to try to understand what is going on.

'Normally at the beginning of the year Michael has many more tests with the new car than I do, but this year when I had the new car it was wet. Then you say, okay, but in Australia you went just about the same speed, so what happened since? It's difficult to say, but I think that Michael was up to the limit of the car quicker than I was.'

The talk in 2003 was that the F2003-GA was a harder car to set up, which was why Barrichello often got it going so well. And that the F2004's shorter wheelbase made it a little more edgy on the limit. Rather than get into a discussion about that, however, he pointed out the characteristics of the F2004. 'It is definitely a quicker car and definitely an easier car to drive, but there is more limit in terms of finding one step, and then finding another one in the right direction. We started differently. It's a bit strange, and the tyres didn't always have an open window.'

He was, he inferred, a victim of his own desire to pursue every potential avenue of greater performance. There was also the issue of left-foot braking. He had never liked it in the past, but Michael did and some suggested that was an area in which he had an advantage. 'No,' Barrichello countered, 'I am braking with both feet. I tried it in '95 and it didn't work. It is true to say that I've tried it on some other tracks and it did work, but now I'm definitely using both.' But he was choosing when and where to do that. The word was that left-foot braking had finally helped him to find the answer to ultra speed through the Spoon Curve and 130R at Suzuka the previous year.

Despite Schumacher's runaway successes, he said at the Nürburgring that he wasn't too worried about 2004 slipping away. 'The way that things were going last year I still had better chances of winning the championship with Ferrari. It's just another win away. A win here would make it start to be my race again. My team is doing a good job for me, my engineers, but we need to be a little bit more precise putting the car together because as I said the window is a little bit smaller. Michael has been a little bit quicker than me, so I need to find a little bit more. It's not that he is quicker, but the line where the car is ... If I am complaining about understeer with the same set-up, he isn't. That's something that is annoying.'

Their driving styles differed, he said. 'For the right foot and the left foot, it's very different.'

And when he was asked whether left-foot braking suited a very pointy car, one which had tremendous front-end grip and therefore tended to oversteer a lot, which was always taken to be the way that Schumacher best liked his cars to be, he made an interesting point. 'Michael doesn't drive a car that is very oversteery, like people think. Maybe he used to. But now he likes a car that is balanced, much as I do. It's just that this year, for the same set-up, I'm having a little bit more understeer than him and I'm having to be tricky with some other stuff.'

Despite all the problems and relative disappointments – after all, going into the Nürburgring he already had 38 championship points – he remained even more convinced than ever that he could beat his teammate after performances such as Silverstone and Suzuka.

'I'm a racing driver racing against him, so I have to believe that way. People will eventually say it's ridiculous, how can you think that way? Michael has proved himself so many times now. But, you know, it's just a matter of ourselves believing in ourselves when we are driving the car. As I've told you before, I have so much belief in myself. Michael doesn't have anything more than I have. Okay, you could have a situation where it's just one engine per weekend, so that's the best one will go to him, but mine will be within half a horsepower, so that's not a problem. It's just a question that the team works for him in a way that I don't think anyone would ever have thought about. He has so much support, but I am inside the team and I have to work.'

That was not frustrating, he remarked, the knowledge that Schumacher could always inspire in others that little bit extra, 'Because I keep on thinking that if I beat him I can keep on doing it.'

But that relied, of course, on him being allowed to beat Schumacher. Team orders might have been banned officially after 2002, but there was nothing the FIA or anyone else could do to change a team's inherent philosophy...

'I keep thinking there's something on the car set-up that I'm trying to do differently, trying to get the situation where I can find good things for myself and then beat him. But the car is not allowing me to do that. We end up pretty close on set-up, and Michael is the one to take advantage in qualifying and with one or two positions in front he is having different races. That's all I can think.'

It was an interesting answer, but it did not come close to answering the age-old question: in a fair fight, was he ever going to be allowed to beat Michael?

It was not something that arose in Germany, where he survived attack by a hungry Sato in the first corner when, quite frankly, it seemed that the optimistic Japanese driver rather caught him unawares as he temporarily grabbed second place before having to pit for a new front wing after damaging his original barging through. In a slightly battered car, Barrichello soldiered on to finish nearly 18 seconds behind Schumacher and only a handful ahead of Button.

'I thought Sato's move was a bit amateur,' he said. 'Luckily I just saw his nose and moved over.'

Things were better in Canada, where, once the BMW Williamses had been disqualified for brake duct regulation infringements, he finished second again to Michael with fastest lap after they had apparently raced one another throughout. 'It made me a little bit anxious,' Ross Brawn admitted, 'because you could see all the scenarios, and if the drivers had tangled then two lead Ferraris would have been out of the race! That would have made a good headline.'

'It was frustrating not being able to get past Michael,' Barrichello said. 'I knew he had a little bit more fuel than I did initially and I had only one real chance to pass and Michael was fair keeping his line and I came on the inside. I thought for one moment that I had him, because I was alongside, but I had a little lower grip than him there and he managed to hold it sideways and make the chicane. It was very much on the limit and I don't think I could have done it any different.'

Then he celebrated with his first pole position of the season in Indianapolis a week later. That race also went Michael's way, however, and he led Rubens home by 2.9 seconds. On that occasion fastest lap was not a consolation.

'I am happy to leave North America with 16 points,' he said, 'but a little bit disappointed as I felt I could have won both here and in Canada. My car was excellent today, but when the safety car came in [after a major accident to Ralf Schumacher] my tyre pressures were too low and I got wheelspin in the final corner, which is why Michael was able to slipstream past me and get past as I could not close the door. I also lost some positions in my first pit stop, but I was pushing really hard. I also hit something hard on the track, some debris, and thought I had broken the suspension. Eventually I was able to attack Michael again after my final stop, but he closed the door fairly.'

Magny-Cours and Silverstone yielded only a brace of thirds, with Alonso and Räikkönen respectively beating him. He drove well in France after a hydraulic problem left him only tenth on the grid on a track where overtaking is notoriously hard. The highlight was pouncing on the hapless Trulli, who slowed too much in Turn 13 on the final lap, which enabled Barrichello to get alongside in Turn 15 and grab the final podium slot. 'I didn't want to make it tenth to fourth and then crash so I was trying 85 per cent, and when I saw I had a chance I added another 20 per cent to make it 105 per cent!'

At Silverstone Ferrari chose an aggressive strategy for him and more conservative one for Michael as the latter was struggling a little, but in the race it turned out that the conservative strategy was better so Barrichello had a tough time fighting to match Räikkönen's pace.

He failed to score at Hockenheim, where he finished only 12th after breaking his front wing trying to protect his line from attack by Montoya and ending up clobbering Coulthard.

Thus far, then, 2004 had been an up-and-down year in which he struggled for genuine consistency. If Michael was winning everything, after all, it was reasonable to expect the other Ferrari to keep following him home, and it wasn't.

They finished 1–2 in Hungary to secure Ferrari the constructors' title, with Michael taking off from pole and once again appearing to have made a superior tyre choice. His latest run of success finally came to an end when Räikkönen staged a brilliant revival for McLaren Mercedes to beat the champion fair and square on the superfast Spa-Francorchamps circuit in Belgium. This time Barrichello was third, four seconds behind his team leader, who finally ended the Brazilian's mathematical chance of the title by putting it beyond his points reach.

The bald facts hid drama, however. After the weather mixed up the grid, there was carnage at the start as Webber crashed into the back of Barrichello's car, causing a puncture and damaging the wing. However, a series of incidents through the race which brought out the safety car helped him to work back into contention and he was delighted with a podium finish. 'At the moment it is hard for me to think straight,' he admitted afterwards,' finishing third after what happened at the start. 'It's a magic feeling!'

His real change in fortune finally came in the best possible place (at least, for a Ferrari driver), when Barrichello took pole position at Monza after a brilliant qualifying lap, and beat Michael (who had crashed very heavily at the track in testing the previous week) by 1.347 seconds. For whatever reason, he was not asked to get out of the way this time. It was not an easy win, however, as the race began on a wet surface and the first tyre stops happened after only five laps. By that point Barrichello had built a lead of 6.9 seconds.

'It was a difficult decision when to stop, because the sun was out and it was going to dry, but it was difficult to know when. I thought that on wets I could open a gap in the first five laps and then stop, but over the radio it was a bit of a mess to know when to do it. I think in the end it was a lap too long, but everything worked out very well. There was a point in the race where I thought everything was lost because Michael overtook me, Antonio Pizzonia overtook me [having replaced the injured Ralf Schumacher at BMW Williams] and I had actually taken a gamble in qualifying and gone a little towards wet setting and here it was drying out. But as the fuel went down my car became faster and faster and I was able to push again and to win.'

It was his speed in preparation for his third and final fuel stop that proved decisive, and which would get him back on track before Schumacher could challenge again. 'I just kept pushing and pushing and didn't see anything. I was telling myself "You deserve this, just push the throttle down, just go as fast as you can". So when I came out of the pits I had no one in front and no one behind. So I kept asking over the radio, "Which position am I in? Which position am I in?" And they came back and said, "P1". Then I said something in Portuguese which I can't repeat! It was just a phenomenal feeling.'

For the first time since 2002, he followed up with another victory, this time as the circus moved to Shanghai for the inaugural Chinese Grand Prix. Having started from pole position again, he was all that stood between Jenson Button and his first Grand Prix win and BAR Honda's first, but though Button pushed as hard as he knew how Barrichello had an answer to every attack the Briton made and, coincidentally, beat him by exactly the same margin he had beaten Michael at Monza.

'I had a very good start and was amazed by the grip on the first lap. Actually, because I underestimated it I could have pushed a little bit harder, which felt really, really nice. It was hard because of the pressure from Kimi and Jenson, and though towards the end I had an eight second gap and wasn't pushing too much because of the danger of graining the front tyres, that was giving me a tougher time towards the finish. I also had two cars to lap, and the first time I went to pass Villeneuve he didn't see me and I lost a second. But it was okay and here I am. It's been a fabulous weekend and it feels good to have made some history in China.'

Barrichello's polished performance was a contrast to Schumacher's drive that day. The champion didn't quite sink to Suzuka 2003 levels, but he was in a foul mood all weekend. After spinning in qualifying and having to start at the back of the grid (Ferrari actually started him from the pit lane just to avoid any possible start-line tangles), his race was compromised by a collision with the Jaguar driven by Austrian rookie Christian Klien, then a spin, and finally a puncture which left him a lapped 12th. There was plenty of speculation as to what was going on in his head, and the favourite answer was that he had learned of a team principals' meeting in which a show of hands had tentatively agreed to a single-tyre rule for 2005 onwards.

Barrichello's superb performances cemented his second place in the drivers' championship, but when they all got to Suzuka, Michael demoralised everyone again with a pole position won on Sunday morning after Saturday's practice and qualifying had been cancelled due to the threat from a local typhoon which, fortunately, veered away from Suzuka at the last moment.

Schumacher won the race with ease, but Barrichello's chances ended when he and old sparring partner David Coulthard collided in the chicane.

This long and grinding season finally ended in Interlagos, where Barrichello raised hopes with a strong pole position. Montoya joined him on the front row with a hungry Räikkönen next up and Schumacher way down the grid in 18th place after he had been forced to switch to the spare Ferrari having crashed his intended race car in a heavy accident in qualifying. That lost him ten grid places because a change of car amounted to a change of engine, but in any case his time would only have been good enough for an eighth place start.

Barrichello had gone to Brazil feeling very optimistic.

'For the very first time I was lucky that I didn't test between the races, so I was able to come straight to Brazil and I got here on the Monday right after Japan, so I was able to stay with my family. I was able to capitalise a little bit on the time difference because it took me two or three days to get going on the sleeping, because in between China and Japan I stayed over there, so I was on different timing for over 20 days. I've been training quite hard, because Interlagos physically is not easy, but I've also been playing football with Michael. I scored a goal and Michael scored on a penalty, which is quite different ...'

There was a hint of nostalgia, too, for Senna's nephew Bruno would demonstrate one of his late uncle's Lotus F1 cars. 'I think many people will be coming to the race circuit to see the race,' Barrichello said, 'but many of them will have the pleasure to see that car running again. It's definitely a plus that Senna's car will be driven again. I wish I could drive it ...'

He looked relaxed and confident, and was clearly relishing the season finale taking place in his own backyard. 'For me this used to be a good grand prix always, but there used to be pressure. In all the phases that I've gone through in my life, especially after

Jordan, I had to change my attitude and I had to send the emotions away from everything that I do. I was actually joking with one of our Italian friends, saying that you don't have to believe in things: just because I haven't finished the last ten races, it doesn't mean that I won't finish again. I have to remember the good times. I don't believe in bad luck at all.

'So the weekend is just nice. I have a lot of work to do. I've been with the press for a long time now. Actually this is probably the first time that I've been speaking in English this weekend! I've just finished one press conference in Portuguese about five minutes ago. But it's a race I enjoy and it's a race where after a hard day's work I can go back home and sleep in my bed. It's just so good.'

He was not, however, expecting any favours from Schumacher, whom he had upstaged in Italy and China but who had hit back in Japan a fortnight earlier. 'To be very honest, it's just like we are with Ricardo [Zonta], Montoya, Alonso and so on. Whenever he's racing in his own place, you hope that the guy does well. It would have been lovely for Sato to finish on the podium in Japan. I think this is the same. At the bottom of his heart, Michael would like for me to finish quite well here, but if he had to decide whether he was going to win or let me win, I'm sure he would choose for himself to win. So I'm not expecting any presents. And I don't want any presents. I'm feeling as good as ever. I'm lucky that I can be here with a competitive car, in the state of mind that I'm feeling right now, just feeling good, and I'm just putting it in first gear tomorrow and just seeing my people and going for it. It's a lovely racing track for me. I think it's one of the best in terms of overtaking. I'm feeling good. Is this the time I can win? I've no idea and I don't care. We're going to see on Sunday afternoon and it's just that it will depend much on me and much on the team that is putting in so much effort and giving me the chance to go for it.

'To be honest, however, if I got to Brazil without any wins, feeling that this was the last race and trying to do that here, it would have been very difficult, in terms of just a pure mind game. It would have been very difficult. So I think those two race wins were fantastic. The Japanese Grand Prix was a bit of a problem in terms of everything, but I had the speed to win there as well if it wasn't for the qualifying. Those two races certainly promoted a good state of mind. After Michael won the championship, I think the team relaxed in a way that gave the chance for both drivers to have a win. The team is giving me a VIP feeling, so I'm feeling good.'

Yet again, however, Barrichello's home race played him false. Jim Clark, Nigel Mansell, and Alain Prost could seemingly win at home at will in days gone by, but somehow it has never yet clicked for Barrichello at Interlagos. While Schumacher worked through to finish seventh as Montoya narrowly beat Räikkönen, Barrichello's big dream of a victory at home failed to materialise yet again. He led off the line on a track made greasy by light pre-race rain, but by Turn Three Räikkönen had moved ahead. Rubens repassed the McLaren on the fourth lap as Räikkönen, Montoya, Trulli, and Schumacher pitted for dry tyres. Barrichello pitted two laps later but was now down in eighth place, most importantly of all behind Montoya and Räikkönen, who both looked particularly strong. His second stop put him ahead of Alonso and Ralf Schumacher and into the third place he would occupy at the finish. It was his best-ever performance at home, but not quite the result he wanted.

'The circumstances today didn't favour us,' he said philosophically. 'I could not have done better. So I can still leave here with my head held high, even if that may actually be difficult because my neck is hurting a lot and I have to admit that I feel very tired. Maybe it was the stress of the whole weekend. I'm happy to be on the podium, even if the win is still to come for me here.'

In the middle of the season Ferrari announced that it had re-signed Barrichello for two further seasons, taking his contract, like Schumacher's, to the end of 2006 and finally ending rumours that he might be looking elsewhere. All of the negotiations had been made behind closed doors, and he admitted that he was privately appalled by the hoopla surrounding Button's attempt (which was ultimately thwarted by the Contract Recognition Board) to move from BAR to Williams for 2005. 'First of all, I would have resolved the matter inside closed doors,' he said. 'I wouldn't have told the press what I wanted to do before anything went to the public, because for me, it would have been much more simple. Secondly, I think that it's very hard to drive for a team if you wish for another one. It's just like having a girlfriend that you don't want any more, you want the other one. What do you do? I want to kiss that one, but this one is sticking with me. It's all a bit of a difficult situation ...'

He and his manager, Fred della Noce, did not agree sufficiently lucrative terms anywhere else, leaving the way clear to negotiate a new contract with Ferrari believed to be worth around $15 million. After the manner in which, in 2003, he had often got more out of his car than his illustrious teammate, it was a sensible choice, and former Ferrari champion Niki Lauda, who is renowned for speaking his mind at all times, had complimentary things to say.

'When he is faced with a "funny" car, Rubens can get more out of it than Michael,' meaning that Barrichello is better at setting up a difficult machine to get the best from it. With his seven wins, nine pole positions and 11 fastest race laps, he was far and away Schumacher's most successful partner.

'Rubens is always underrated,' Ferrari technical director Ross Brawn said. 'But he is always a valued member of the team. Many times Michael has adopted Rubens's set-up. The short practice before qualifying in 2003 obliged us sometimes to have the drivers following different paths, and then we chose the best one. Rubens's contribution was even more important in 2003 and we have always been totally confident in everything that he's done. He has always contributed at a high level.'

Jean Todt, Ferrari's sporting director, said: 'We are very happy with Rubens. He impressed a lot and we did not see any particular reasons not to move forward as we are.'

These were, to some extent, the sort of comments you would expect any team to make about one of their drivers, whether they were retaining him or bidding him a fond farewell. But by 2004 Barrichello really had begun to sway over the doubters within the team, and on a personal level his relationships within Maranello were as strong as ever.

There were some, however, who believed he had been persuaded to stay simply on financial grounds, having been unable to agree better terms elsewhere. That's not exactly a crime, but as he elected to stay aboard Barrichello explained his thinking in an interview with the *crash.net* website.

'Let me say this. If a team is happy with its drivers, in that case it is easy to stay with its drivers. It's easier for the team's car, because it allows the team to develop the car even further. If you change two drivers, everything has to be started from scratch. Maybe one driver worked with a car which understeered and then you have a new driver and you have an oversteering car, so it becomes difficult. First you have to go backwards and then you can go forwards. So those that kept their drivers did the best deal because it allows the team to really develop the car. But of course, this doesn't mean that they are going to get the best results, so at the end, I think that for example within Ferrari we really have a good team and we can work on what we need. We don't have to create new things or invent new things. We simply have to work on the problems that we have and at testing at Jerez, for instance, in those couple of days I saw what was necessary on the car (for 2005's new regulations), but I'm sure that for Barcelona the car will have been developed with a step forward. If you have a new driver, he will be saying that I need an extra day to get used to the car. So you can't develop the car, it becomes a bit more difficult if you change drivers.'

He also reacted cleverly when asked if he hadn't become fed up with people asking whether he was really a joint number one driver or merely a number two.

'I'm going to turn that question around and try to answer it. What can I say? I'm always there, I'm always fully committed. If, one day, I should start thinking and say that "Look, I will never catch Michael", I'm sure that from that day I would not stay at Ferrari because I would lose the motivation to be the best. I still have the motivation to be the best. Whether this will take place this year, or another year, we don't know. It's going to depend on my work, it depends on what I can do, it will depend on how I will adjust to the new rules.

'But these are just words. I have to keep my right foot down, I have to use my head, I have to be as calm as I have been, like I drove in Brazil. I was really happy that I was calm, I drove the car easily, because I really wanted to drive the car because I love what I do, because I have a team behind me which is extremely nice, with all the engineers, my mechanics, everyone, and so really it is all enjoyable from my point. I'm also happy that Michael is in the team because it means that we can push even more, each one pushes the other to go faster.'

Despite the disappointment in Interlagos, the year did end on a high note with a victory at home. In November, Barrichello and his close friend, the newly crowned IRL champion Tony Kanaan, teamed with fellow IRL racers Daniel Wheldon and Felipe Giaffone to win the brutally challenging annual Granja Viana 500 kart race in Brazil. They beat a field of 74 karts and 300 drivers.

Barrichello put his kart on pole position and led from the start until a brake problem arose. After that the quartet had to work their way back to the front, and did so to win by 15 seconds after a gruelling ten and a half hours of racing. Fellow Brazilians Gil de Ferran (the 2001 CART champ), Helio Castroneves, Rubem Carrapatoso, and Oswaldo Negri finished second. And in third place, making it an even sweeter win for Rubinho? A kart driven by Mario Haberfeld, Charlie Fonseca and ... Christian Fittipaldi, which finished seven laps adrift.

Juan Pablo Montoya, the man who had triumphed in the Brazilian Grand Prix which Rubinho had so coveted, dropped back with engine problems, delayed further when younger brother Federico bent an axle after shunting the kart.

It was the fifth time that Barrichello and Kanaan had won, in eight attempts.

'All my teammates deserve great praise,' Barrichello said. 'I had some very satisfying moments this weekend, and putting the kart on pole was awesome.'

Chapter 13

A TITLE RUN AT LAST?
THE FUTURE

It is in the Brazilian nature to see the sunny side and to travel in hope, and Rubens Barrichello proved no exception to his national character as he prepared for the 2005 season. Ever since 2000 he had become used to Michael Schumacher hogging the limelight at Ferrari, yet every season he looked forward to the moment when he could string together in every race the sort of drives that had seen him dominant in Silverstone and Suzuka in 2003, or Monza and Shanghai in 2004.

His critics merely laughed with each optimistic sentence he uttered, but deep in his heart Barrichello continues to believe in himself and his potential. But take away Schumacher, quite the most extraordinary driver of his generation, and Barrichello would have won another 13 races for Ferrari and possibly two world championships, and those are not the statistics of a journeyman, especially one who has had to contend with such a superlative teammate.

Though he has been criticised for failing to take the fight consistently to Schumacher, or for being the German's 'lackey', staying at Ferrari was his choice for the new season.

He could, however, have gone to BMW Williams instead.

'We talked and put some conversations into prospect, and it got a little bit serious, but not serious enough,' is all he will say on the matter. But sources within Williams suggest that things got quite a long way down the line. They began talking late in 2003, around the time that Barrichello stormed to victory at Suzuka. But before things could get too formalised Williams broke off temporarily in order to focus on its new car. Later talks resumed in mid-2004, but it is thought that an offer of $8 million did not prove attractive to a man thought to be earning a lot more than that at Ferrari.

It wasn't the first time that the Brazilian had held talks with top-line British teams. In 1994 he came very close to joining McLaren.

'It's hard to understand why it went wrong,' Barrichello says now. 'Initially I was very highly rated with McLaren, but over a three-month period that thing went down and the talks weren't there. I felt bad about it. All of a sudden Ron [Dennis] was saying maybe we should wait a bit. I had signed an option, but I still don't know what went wrong. Something else happened, or Ron was too happy with Mika. I don't know. I wasn't asking too much, and all of a sudden we were in Japan and Ron was saying we should wait and released me from the option. That was that. But I'm sure that, inside, he still rates me high. I thought being sixth in the Championship that year was not bad, in a Jordan ...'

Williams and BAR came knocking for 1999, but the get-out clause in his Stewart contract proved insurmountable. 'I think I had too big a bill to pay,' he now says with a smile. 'With Frank things were available, so it was a mutual thing. Initially, I don't think Frank thought my contract was firm, which it was. I had an option, but it was firm. The same way that Jackie rates me high, I rate him high, so in the back of my mind I knew that he was going to win. And that he was going to do it sooner than it took Jordan to win. That was for sure.'

The ever-present influence of Ayrton Senna has helped to mature him. And to understand what makes him the man he is you have to appreciate just what Senna meant to him. In June 1999 memories of his hero, mentor, and friend came flooding back when he was invited to Goodwood's Festival of Speed. Initially he was to drive a Lotus 79 – 'Emotional enough for me, because it was the first racing car I ever remember seeing in action, lying on the floor of my grandmother's house watching it on television.' But the icing on the cake was the chance to run the McLaren MP4/6 raced previously by Senna.

That visit to Goodwood, then, would be a charged pilgrimage, for an openly emotional man. 'When Honda heard I was going, they asked Lord March if I'd like to drive the McLaren. I said, "Oh yes, yes, yes!"

'When I sat in the car it said "Scrutineered April 2, 1992", and that year I was in F3000 and went back to see the race in Brazil. That label meant even more, because here was a car that had actually been scrutineered for Ayrton to race there. I was finding more and more examples that were emotionally very, very nice. I would drive a car that Ayrton had driven in Brazil.

'It was just nice to sit in the car, amazing. I am a very cheerful person, and though all the time in the car I felt emotional, I was pretty much in control. Four years earlier I probably would have cried. But most of all I just felt special. Jo Ramirez from McLaren came to talk to me, and that was special too because of his relationship with Ayrton. I think he was quite emotional as well, which meant a lot to me. It was nice when he told me that Ayrton used to love that particular steering wheel. I really liked it too, because it was made specially for him. It was also nice that the guy who strapped me in told me that Ayrton was the last guy he had done that to in that car. Everything felt as if it had its place, you know?'

An incident involving the car and British driver Jonathan Palmer ultimately prevented Barrichello from driving the McLaren more than once, 'but doing just one run maybe made it even more special. I felt that the whole thing was a gift from God, because I've been outside that car, looking at Ayrton, wishing I could be driving it one day. And here I was! I couldn't let it go without driving full throttle, so I went full throttle in second gear going up, and then even though I didn't keep full revs I used every gear so I could say I had done that. When I got to the top of the hill I just thought, "Thank God. Thank everyone for the opportunity." Because it was fantastic.'

Barrichello is unashamedly sentimental, especially where Senna is concerned. 'I really do think that he is an angel, and he's alongside God and even now he is looking after me.'

Perhaps because of that, he clearly enjoys his role as Brazil's motorsport elder statesman, and there is nothing contrived about his support for his upcoming fellow countrymen. Just as Senna once helped him, so he is happy to reach a hand down to help others. The mantle has been passed down. In the press conference on the Thursday before the Brazilian Grand Prix in 2004, he sat alongside Ricardo Zonta, who was having his final grand prix with Toyota after standing in when Cristiano da Matta left the team mid-season. 'I'm so happy for Ricardo that he's here,' Barrichello began, 'because when they said that Jarno [Trulli] was joining, it was probably a nice thing for Toyota, but as Ricardo had a chance to drive in some grands prix, this is probably the best one for him to do. I'm not saying it because Ricardo is here, but I've always said to the press that I didn't think he had a real chance to drive at BAR [back in 1999]. I think there was too much pressure and probably the time there with Jacques [Villeneuve] wasn't good at all. When I saw him behind me and pushing me in Spa this year, I wanted to protect my position, but when I saw smoke [from Zonta's engine, which expired with a lap to go when he was running fourth], I really wished that it wasn't him because he deserved the points there. I think he does have a place in Formula One, and people should take him a little more seriously.'

Then there's the mercurial Felipe Massa, the young Brazilian whose heart sometimes still rules his head but who exudes great charisma. He and Barrichello worked together when Massa left Sauber Petronas in 2002 and spent a year as Ferrari's test driver before rejoining the Swiss team for 2004.

'Felipe matured quite a lot inside Ferrari. He has still had an up-and-down season in 2004 with Giancarlo [Fisichella]. In terms of speed, I think he matched Giancarlo quite well. In terms of pure results, it was a bit difficult because of all the problems he had but he has the talent, so if he has a good set-up in terms of mind management and progresses, just keeps on going, he's going to have a good year and probably he can win races in the future.'

Barrichello helped Massa a great deal at Ferrari, where another young Brazilian, former Jaguar and Prost racer Luciano Burti, also played a test role. 'I tried to have Luciano in the team because he was a good test driver, he was a good race driver too, so it was good for him to be there and it was nice to have Felipe. Obviously he's quite young, so when he came he was trying to learn all the time and all the things that he asked me, I managed to answer, no problem.'

There are, however, times when he does not shrink from speaking his mind, and the new regulations for 2005 were a case in point. Barrichello was assuredly not happy about the prospect of using only one set of tyres per race weekend.

'I expect the car to be slower, certainly, but we're trying to prepare ourselves well to gain back everything that we lose with the new rules,' he said, referring to aerodynamic changes which had initially reduced downforce. 'It will slide around more, lose some braking power going into the corners and some grip through them and pick-up coming out, but it will still be fun to drive. But the main factor will be that we are going to have one tyre for the whole weekend, which I don't think Formula One is prepared for. I don't think it's a good idea. I'm sorry to be direct about that, but when I was a karter I didn't dream of Formula One racing on one tyre. The tyre manufacturers want to win races and they will take everything to its limit, to be quick and reliable. But maybe someone could suffer, from testing or anything. Although I'm such a believer that we're going to get to the end with Bridgestone, setting up everything, it might be too early for that in 2005 and I'm a little bit afraid in terms of safety. So I'm not in favour of the one tyre rule. I'm in favour of the new engine rule, where it has to last two races. That seems to be okay and if you have a failure, you have to change engines and lose ten positions.

It might make a better show for Formula One, that's okay. But one set of tyres? I used to race one tyre per year in go-kart because I didn't have money but that's a completely different thing!'

This is ironic, because of all the drivers his style is the best suited to a new era in which preservation of your tyres is going to play a key role. 'If you flat-spot a tyre, for instance, that's it. Game over. I've been really happy with the work that Bridgestone has been doing since Suzuka and Interlagos, and the tyres will last a lot longer and we will take a step forward in some areas. But I can tell you, this year we will have to use our heads a lot more than our feet with these new regulations.'

Above all, Rubens Barrichello seems a happy man. In January 2005 he achieved a long-held ambition when, together with Michael Schumacher and members of the Ferrari team, he went to the Vatican to be received by the Pope. He is content with his lot at Ferrari and will never give up his quest to beat Michael Schumacher, regardless of whether others doubt he will succeed.

'I was worried when he talked to Williams,' Eddie Jordan said. 'His heart has always seemed to be with Ferrari, and who else in recent seasons could have helped him to achieve what he has? He went there and he learned to play the long game. Eddie Irvine didn't, and he couldn't cope. Rubens has tactical genius and he's not soft and defeatist. Can he beat Michael? Truthfully, I don't think anyone in Formula One right now can beat him consistently, he is such a great package. But Rubens can do it on occasion and on his day he is as good as anyone else out there.'

'Rubens is a nice little bloke,' says Peter Collins, whose talent-spotting ability furthered the Formula One careers of Nigel Mansell, Johnny Herbert, Mika Häkkinen, Alex Zanardi and, more recently, Kimi Räikkönen and Vitantonio Liuzzi. 'He drives beautifully, with polish and grace, but maybe he doesn't have that last ounce of speed. He is ultimately not tough enough. Other drivers know that he will be in there when the car is right, but none of them tremble when they see it is him; it's not the same as knowing it's Michael or Kimi in their mirrors.'

Long-time friend Gary Anderson offered another view. 'When someone who believes in themselves gets an offer to drive for Ferrari it would be difficult to say no, and for Rubens that was everything he wished for. He sat down with Jackie and myself and told us of the offer and we fully backed him, but tried to make him aware that one MS was not going to be easy. Perhaps he could beat him but would the infrastructure allow this to happen? I don't think so, I think that answers the question of Rubens becoming world champion at Ferrari. If he was to move on then I have no doubt that he has the ability, but do any of the other teams have the ability at the moment? Again, unless Ferrari or Bridgestone really trip up then I can't see it in the next couple of years ...

'We are still very good friends, his mum makes very good fishwada and I have enjoyed it at his home. I have a lovely picture of Michael, Rubens, and myself in the Log Cabin at Suzuka at the end of 2003 at about five in the morning, all feeling a little worse of the wear ...'

Barrichello is nonetheless calmer about things than he has ever been. In the overall scheme of things in the world, does it really matter whether he beats Michael Schumacher? Yes it does, of course, because that is the aim of every race driver, yet, equally, no it doesn't. The real losers in life are the snipers and the armchair critics, not the men who get down into the dust of the arena and give it their best shot.

'My humour is changing much less, winning or not winning,' he says. 'I am taking the gratitude of knowing I did the best I could on that particular day. But I am not stopping. People can say whatever they think and they can criticise, but it's my life and I am gonna keep on going. Formula One can change so much, but so long as you keep your feet on the ground you are the same guy. My son Eduardo has helped me to open up my perspective. More often I want to be with him, that's for sure, and I wanna do more racing than testing because the testing takes me away from home. The racing is okay because I can actually take him, but testing, there's no way to take your family to that. You are inside the car doing 600 kilometres because somebody decided you can only have one engine per weekend. And for that one engine per weekend thing to work, you gotta be doing 600, 700 kilometres a day to see if the engine can last the whole weekend.

'It is a bit frustrating, to be honest. Because what's the reason to be driving in Formula One? You dream all your life to be driving a Formula One car, and at the end of a 700-odd kilometre day you are knackered and you don't love Formula One any more. It's just the next day that you start loving it again. So there is a limit...'

Eduardo was three in September 2004, and Barrichello is a doting father. His face broadens into an even larger grin whenever Eduardo's name is mentioned. 'Want to see a photograph of him?' 'Family life?' he asks. 'It's fantastic! My son is wonderful. The way he talks is just phenomenal. We are having a wonderful time. He is very much into model racing. I don't know, maybe all the kids are and I hope that's true, because at two-and-a-half years he could hit a golf ball 40 yards. I am amazed how much these kids can do. He knows how to do it, but he's saying, "Daddy, like this? Like this?" And then bang! When eventually he hits the ball, it's just so nice to see it! So we are having a very, very good time. When I got to Brazil before the race in 2004 it was fantastic to spend time with my family – I had been over 20 days without seeing my son. We had a chance to play, and Sylvana said she didn't know which one was the kid...'

The family wheel may yet turn full circle. If Eduardo Barrichello wants to get behind the wheel, his father has indicated he will not stand in his way. 'It's his life,' he answers immediately. 'I'll support him, the way my father supported me. My father was with us for Monte Carlo, and again in Brazil. The day I was 32, he was 54. We have always been very close. He is just loving having a grandson! And if Eduardo wants to race... okay! I hope I can do for him what my father did for me.'

In the meantime, Rubens Barrichello races on himself. Sometimes he wins, and on his day he can beat anyone, including

Michael Schumacher. But win or lose, he always behaves with dignity and his charm rarely reaches breaking point. And being the emotional type, there is rarely any confusion about what he is thinking.

And he is honest enough to admit that he can learn things from his son, like he did after Monaco in 2004 where he finished third but scowled on the podium. 'He asked me afterwards why I wasn't smiling, I was on the podium. And it really got to me because I realised that I should have been smiling. I had achieved something. He taught me that.'

And that's why you won't ever see him *not* smiling from now on whenever he's on the podium.

Most of all, he dreams of that time when, as one of the sport's good guys, he will have his day in the sun. Perhaps even win that elusive title. 'When I die,' he once said, 'I hope people will say of me, "After all he's been through, he took a bit longer but in the end he did it."'

As he walks his unenviable tightrope as Michael Schumacher's partner, knowing that he *can* beat him but not yet always, he remains driven by that inner belief in himself and in the inherent fairness of life. Do right by others, and somehow, someday, life will ultimately do right by you.

It may be naïve thinking and the inherent vulnerability of that line of thought is further ammunition to his critics, but in its own way it is as endearing as his innate character itself. It explains why he is one of the most genuinely popular drivers that a hard-nosed sport has seen in the last decade. Just ask a young kid in Montreal, or the countless other fans who have benefited from his charm.

Rubinho brings to mind a wonderful epitaph one of her friends penned for the late Lynda Lee-Potter, the greatest national newspaper columnist of her time. 'If she liked you, she liked you,' they said. 'And if she didn't, it was your fault.'

Rubens Barrichello's
Results

Key: FL = fastest lap; Pole = pole position;
DNF = did not finish; DNQ = did not qualify;
DNS = did not start; DSQ = disqualified.

1981
Sao Paulo Junior Karting Championship: 2nd

1982
Sao Paulo Junior Karting Championship: 2nd
Brazilian National Junior Karting Championship: 9th

1983
Sao Paulo Junior Karting Championship: Winner of
  championship
Brazilian National Junior Karting Championship: Winner of
  championship
Brazilian Amateur Driver of the Year Award (voted by Olympic
  Committee)

1984
Sao Paulo Junior Karting Championship: 2nd
Brazilian National Junior Karting Championship: Winner of
  championship

1985

Sao Paulo Karting Championship – Category B: Winner of championship

Brazilian National Karting Championship: 4th

Duas Horas de Interlagos Endurance Challenge: Champion

1986

Sao Paulo Karting Championship – Category A: Winner of championship

Brazilian National Karting Championship – Category A: Winner of championship

1987

Sao Paulo Karting Championship – Category A: Winner of championship

Brazilian National Karting Championship – Category A: Winner of championship

South American Karting Championship: Winner of championship

World Karting Championship: 9th

1988

Sao Paulo (Region) Karting Championship – Category A: Winner of championship

Sao Paulo (City) Karting Championship – Category A: Winner of championship

Brazilian National Karting Championship – Category A: Winner of championship

Metropolitano Karting Tournament: Winner

1989

Brazilian Formula Ford 1600 Championship: 4th

1990

GM Opel Lotus Euroseries: Winner of championship
Participated in Brazilian Formula Three races in preparation for
   British Formula Three
(fourth, second, and first in three races)

1991

West Surrey Racing, British Formula Three, Ralt RT35 Mugen

17 March	SILVERSTONE CLUB: Pole, DNF
1 April	THRUXTON: Pole, 1st, FL
21 April	DONINGTON PARK GP: DNF
28 April	BRANDS HATCH GP: 3rd
19 May	BRANDS HATCH INDY: 4th
27 May	THRUXTON: Pole, 2nd, FL
9 June	SILVERSTONE CLUB: Pole, 2nd, FL
23 June	DONINGTON PARK GP: Pole, 1st
29 June	SILVERSTONE CLUB: 5th
13 July	SILVERSTONE GP: DNF, FL
4 August	SNETTERTON: 4th, FL
26 August	SILVERSTONE CLUB: 5th
1 September	BRANDS HATCH GP: 3rd, FL
15 September	DONINGTON PARK GP: Pole, 1st, FL
6 October	SILVERSTONE GP: Pole, 1st, FL
13 October	THRUXTON: Pole, 5th

Winner of championship, 74 points (2nd David Coulthard 66)

24 November MACAU (non-championship): 5th

1992

Il Baronne Rampante, Formula 3000, Reynard 92D Judd; Reynard 92D Cosworth

10 May	SILVERSTONE: 2nd, FL
8 June	PAU: 3rd
21 June	BARCELONA: 2nd
12 July	ENNA: DNF
25 July	HOCKENHEIM: 6th
23 August	NÜRBURGRING: 3rd, FL
29 August	SPA-FRANCORCHAMPS: 5th
13 September	ALBACETE: 6th
11 October	NOGARO: 6th
18 October	MAGNY-COURS: 5th

3rd in championship, 27 points (1st Luca Badoer 46, 2nd Andrea Montermini 34)

Edenbridge Racing, Formula Three, Ralt RT36 Mugen

November MACAU: 7th

1993

Jordan Grand Prix, Formula One, Jordan Hart 193

SOUTH AFRICAN GP, KYALAMI
Rubens Barrichello: DNF; Ivan Capelli: DNF

BRAZILIAN GP, INTERLAGOS
Rubens Barrichello: DNF; Ivan Capelli: DNQ

EUROPEAN GP, DONINGTON PARK
Rubens Barrichello: 10th; Thierry Boutsen: DNF

SAN MARINO GP, IMOLA
Rubens Barrichello: DNF; Thierry Boutsen: DNF

SPANISH GP, BARCELONA
Rubens Barrichello: 12th; Thierry Boutsen: 11th

MONACO GP, MONTE CARLO
Rubens Barrichello: 9th; Thierry Boutsen: DNF

CANADIAN GP, MONTREAL
Rubens Barrichello: 9th; Thierry Boutsen: 12th

FRENCH GP, MAGNY-COURS
Rubens Barrichello: 7th; Thierry Boutsen: 11th

BRITISH GP, SILVERSTONE
Rubens Barrichello: 10th; Thierry Boutsen: DNF

GERMAN GP, HOCKENHEIM
Rubens Barrichello: DNF; Thierry Boutsen: 13th

HUNGARIAN GP, HUNGARORING
Rubens Barrichello: DNF; Thierry Boutsen: 9th

BELGIAN GP, SPA-FRANCORCHAMPS
Rubens Barrichello: DNF; Thierry Boutsen: DNF

ITALIAN GP, MONZA
Rubens Barrichello: DNF; Marco Apicella: DNF

PORTUGUESE GP, ESTORIL
Rubens Barrichello: 13th; Emanuele Naspetti: DNF

JAPANESE GP, SUZUKA
Rubens Barrichello: 5th; Eddie Irvine: 6th

AUSTRALIAN GP, ADELAIDE
Rubens Barrichello: 11th; Eddie Irvine: DNF

17th in championship, 2 points (1st Alain Prost 99)

1994
Jordan Grand Prix, Formula One, Jordan Hart 194

BRAZILIAN GP, INTERLAGOS
Rubens Barrichello: 4th; Eddie Irvine: DNF

PACIFIC GP, TI AIDA
Rubens Barrichello: 3rd; Aguri Suzuki: DNF

SAN MARINO GP, IMOLA
Rubens Barrichello: DNS; Andrea de Cesaris: DNF

MONACO GP, MONTE CARLO
Rubens Barrichello: DNF; Andrea de Cesaris: 4th

SPANISH GP, BARCELONA
Rubens Barrichello: DNF; Eddie Irvine: 6th

CANADIAN GP, MONTREAL
Rubens Barrichello: 7th; Eddie Irvine: DNF

FRENCH GP, MAGNY-COURS
Rubens Barrichello: DNF; Eddie Irvine: DNF

BRITISH GP, SILVERSTONE
Rubens Barrichello: 4th; Eddie Irvine: DNS

GERMAN GP, HOCKENHEIM
Rubens Barrichello: DNF; Eddie Irvine: DNF

HUNGARIAN GP, HUNGARORING
Rubens Barrichello: DNF; Eddie Irvine: DNF

BELGIAN GP, SPA-FRANCORCHAMPS
Rubens Barrichello: Pole, DNF; Eddie Irvine: DNF

ITALIAN GP, MONZA
Rubens Barrichello: 4th; Eddie Irvine: DNF

PORTUGUESE GP, ESTORIL
Rubens Barrichello: 4th; Eddie Irvine: 7th

EUROPEAN GP, JEREZ
Rubens Barrichello: 12th; Eddie Irvine: 4th

JAPANESE GP, SUZUKA
Rubens Barrichello: DNF; Eddie Irvine: 5th

AUSTRALIAN GP, ADELAIDE
Rubens Barrichello: 4th; Eddie Irvine: DNF

6th in championship, 19 points (1st Michael Schumacher 92)

1995
Jordan Grand Prix, Formula One, Jordan Peugeot 195

BRAZILIAN GP, INTERLAGOS
Rubens Barrichello: DNF; Eddie Irvine: DNF

ARGENTINIAN GP, BUENOS AIRES
Rubens Barrichello: DNF; Eddie Irvine: DNF

SAN MARINO GP, IMOLA
Rubens Barrichello: DNF; Eddie Irvine: 8th

SPANISH GP, BARCELONA
Rubens Barrichello: 7th; Eddie Irvine: 5th

MONACO GP, MONTE CARLO
Rubens Barrichello: DNF; Eddie Irvine: DNF

CANADIAN GP, MONTREAL
Rubens Barrichello: 2nd; Eddie Irvine: 3rd

FRENCH GP, MAGNY-COURS
Rubens Barrichello: 6th; Eddie Irvine: 9th

BRITISH GP, SILVERSTONE
Rubens Barrichello: 11th; Eddie Irvine: DNF

GERMAN GP, HOCKENHEIM
Rubens Barrichello: DNF; Eddie Irvine: 9th

HUNGARIAN GP, HUNGARORING
Rubens Barrichello: 7th; Eddie Irvine: 13th

BELGIAN GP, SPA-FRANCORCHAMPS
Rubens Barrichello: 6th; Eddie Irvine: DNF

ITALIAN GP, MONZA
Rubens Barrichello: DNF; Eddie Irvine: DNF

PORTUGUESE GP, ESTORIL
Rubens Barrichello: 11th; Eddie Irvine: 10th

EUROPEAN GP, NÜRBURGRING
Rubens Barrichello: 4th; Eddie Irvine: 6th

PACIFIC GP, TI AIDA
Rubens Barrichello: DNF; Eddie Irvine: 11th

JAPANESE GP, SUZUKA
Rubens Barrichello: DNF; Eddie Irvine: 4th

AUSTRALIAN GP, ADELAIDE
Rubens Barrichello: DNF; Eddie Irvine: DNF

11th in championship, 11 points (1st Michael Schumacher 102)

1996
Jordan Grand Prix, Formula One, Jordan Peugeot 196

AUSTRALIAN GP, MELBOURNE
Rubens Barrichello: DNF; Martin Brundle: DNF

BRAZILIAN GP, INTERLAGOS
Rubens Barrichello: DNF; Martin Brundle: 12th

ARGENTINIAN GP, BUENOS AIRES
Rubens Barrichello: 4th; Martin Brundle: DNF

EUROPEAN GP, NÜRBURGRING
Rubens Barrichello: 5th; Martin Brundle: 6th

SAN MARINO GP, IMOLA
Rubens Barrichello: 5th; Martin Brundle: DNF

MONACO GP, MONTE CARLO
Rubens Barrichello: DNF; Martin Brundle: DNF

SPANISH GP, BARCELONA
Rubens Barrichello: DNF; Martin Brundle: DNF

CANADIAN GP, MONTREAL
Rubens Barrichello: DNF; Martin Brundle: 6th

FRENCH GP, MAGNY-COURS
Rubens Barrichello: 9th; Martin Brundle: 8th

BRITISH GP, SILVERSTONE
Rubens Barrichello: 4th; Martin Brundle: 6th

GERMAN GP, HOCKENHEIM
Rubens Barrichello: 6th; Martin Brundle: 10th

HUNGARIAN GP, HUNGARORING
Rubens Barrichello: 6th; Martin Brundle: DNF

BELGIAN GP, SPA-FRANCORCHAMPS
Rubens Barrichello: DNF; Martin Brundle: DNF

ITALIAN GP, MONZA
Rubens Barrichello: 5th; Martin Brundle: 4th

PORTUGUESE GP, ESTORIL
Rubens Barrichello: DNF; Martin Brundle: 9th

JAPANESE GP, SUZUKA
Rubens Barrichello: 9th; Martin Brundle: 5th

8th in championship, 14 points (1st Damon Hill 97)

1997

Stewart Grand Prix, Formula One, Stewart Ford SF-1

AUSTRALIAN GP, MELBOURNE
Rubens Barrichello: DNF; Jan Magnussen: DNF

BRAZILIAN GP, INTERLAGOS
Rubens Barrichello: DNF; Jan Magnussen: DNS

ARGENTINE GP, BUENOS AIRES
Rubens Barrichello: DNF; Jan Magnussen: DNF

SAN MARINO GP, IMOLA
Rubens Barrichello: DNF; Jan Magnussen: DNF

MONACO GP, MONTE CARLO
Rubens Barrichello: 2nd; Jan Magnussen: 7th

SPANISH GP, BARCELONA
Rubens Barrichello: DNF; Jan Magnussen: 13th

CANADIAN GP, MONTREAL
Rubens Barrichello: DNF; Jan Magnussen: DNF

FRENCH GP, MAGNY-COURS
Rubens Barrichello: DNF; Jan Magnussen: DNF

BRITISH GP, SILVERSTONE
Rubens Barrichello: DNF; Jan Magnussen: DNF

GERMAN GP, HOCKENHEIM
Rubens Barrichello: DNF; Jan Magnussen: DNF

HUNGARIAN GP, HUNGARORING
Rubens Barrichello: DNF; Jan Magnussen: DNF

BELGIAN GP, SPA-FRANCORCHAMPS
Rubens Barrichello: DNF; Jan Magnussen: 12th

ITALIAN GP, MONZA
Rubens Barrichello: 13th; Jan Magnussen: DNF

AUSTRIAN GP, A1 RING
Rubens Barrichello: DNF; Jan Magnussen: DNF

GP OF LUXEMBOURG, NÜRBURGRING
Rubens Barrichello: DNF; Jan Magnussen: DNF

JAPANESE GP, SUZUKA
Rubens Barrichello: DNF; Jan Magnussen: DNF

GP OF EUROPE, JEREZ
Rubens Barrichello: DNF; Jan Magnussen: 9th

13th in championship, 6 points (1st Jacques Villeneuve 81)

1998
Stewart Grand Prix, Formula One, Stewart Ford SF-2

AUSTRALIAN GP, MELBOURNE
Rubens Barrichello: DNF; Jan Magnussen: DNF

BRAZILIAN GP, INTERLAGOS
Rubens Barrichello: DNF; Jan Magnussen: 10th

ARGENTINE GP, BUENOS AIRES
Rubens Barrichello: 10th; Jan Magnussen: DNF

SAN MARINO GP, IMOLA
Rubens Barrichello: DNF; Jan Magnussen: DNF

SPANISH GP, BARCELONA
Rubens Barrichello: 5th; Jan Magnussen: 12th

MONACO GP, MONTE CARLO
Rubens Barrichello: DNF; Jan Magnussen: DNF

CANADIAN GP, MONTREAL
Rubens Barrichello: 5th; Jan Magnussen: 6th

FRENCH GP, MAGNY-COURS
Rubens Barrichello: 10th; Jos Verstappen: 12th

BRITISH GP, SILVERSTONE
Rubens Barrichello: DNF; Jos Verstappen: DNF

AUSTRIAN GP, A1 RING
Rubens Barrichello: DNF; Jos Verstappen: DNF

GERMAN GP, HOCKENHEIM
Rubens Barrichello: DNF; Jos Verstappen: DNF

HUNGARIAN GP, HUNGARORING
Rubens Barrichello: DNF; Jos Verstappen: 13th

BELGIAN GP, SPA-FRANCORCHAMPS
Rubens Barrichello: DNS; Jos Verstappen: DNF

ITALIAN GP, MONZA
Rubens Barrichello: 10th; Jos Verstappen: DNF

GP OF LUXEMBOURG, NÜRBURGRING
Rubens Barrichello: 11th; Jos Verstappen: 13th

JAPANESE GP, SUZUKA
Rubens Barrichello: DNF; Jos Verstappen: DNF

12th in championship, 4 points (1st Mika Häkkinen 100)

1999
Stewart Grand Prix, Formula One, Stewart Ford SF-3

AUSTRALIAN GP, MELBOURNE
Rubens Barrichello: 5th; Johnny Herbert: DNS

BRAZILIAN GP, INTERLAGOS
Rubens Barrichello: DNF; Johnny Herbert: DNF

SAN MARINO GP, IMOLA
Rubens Barrichello: 3rd; Johnny Herbert: DNF

MONACO GP, MONTE CARLO
Rubens Barrichello: DNF; Johnny Herbert: DNF

SPANISH GP, BARCELONA
Rubens Barrichello: 8th, DSQ; Johnny Herbert: DNF

CANADIAN GP, MONTREAL
Rubens Barrichello: DNF; Johnny Herbert: 5th

FRENCH GP, MAGNY-COURS
Rubens Barrichello: Pole, 3rd; Johnny Herbert: DNF

BRITISH GP, SILVERSTONE
Rubens Barrichello: 8th; Johnny Herbert: 12th

AUSTRIAN GP, AI-RING
Rubens Barrichello: DNF; Johnny Herbert: 14th

GERMAN GP, HOCKENHEIM
Rubens Barrichello: DNF; Johnny Herbert: 11th

HUNGARIAN GP, HUNGARORING
Rubens Barrichello: 5th; Johnny Herbert: 11th

BELGIAN GP, SPA-FRANCORCHAMPS
Rubens Barrichello: 10th; Johnny Herbert: DNF

ITALIAN GP, MONZA
Rubens Barrichello: 4th; Johnny Herbert: DNF

GP OF EUROPE, NÜRBURGRING
Rubens Barrichello: 3rd; Johnny Herbert: 1st

MALAYSIAN GP, SEPANG
Rubens Barrichello: 5th; Johnny Herbert: 4th

JAPANESE GP, SUZUKA
Rubens Barrichello: 8th; Johnny Herbert: 7th

7th in championship, 21 points (1st Mika Häkkinen 76)

2000
Scuderia Ferrari, Formula One, Ferrari F2000

AUSTRALIAN GP, MELBOURNE
Michael Schumacher: 1st; Rubens Barrichello: 2nd, FL

BRAZILIAN GP, INTERLAGOS
Michael Schumacher: 1st, FL; Rubens Barrichello: DNF

SAN MARINO GP, IMOLA
Michael Schumacher: 1st; Rubens Barrichello: 4th

BRITISH GP, SILVERSTONE
Michael Schumacher: 3rd; Rubens Barrichello: Pole, DNF

SPANISH GP, BARCELONA
Michael Schumacher: 5th; Rubens Barrichello: 3rd

EUROPEAN GP, NÜRBURGRING
Michael Schumacher: 1st, FL; Rubens Barrichello: 4th

MONACO GP, MONTE CARLO
Michael Schumacher: Pole, DNF; Rubens Barrichello: 2nd

CANADIAN GP, MONTREAL
Michael Schumacher: Pole, 1st; Rubens Barrichello: 2nd

FRENCH GP, MAGNY-COURS
Michael Schumacher: Pole, DNF; Rubens Barrichello: 3rd

AUSTRIAN GP, A1-RING
Michael Schumacher: DNF; Rubens Barrichello: 3rd

GERMAN GP, HOCKENHEIM
Michael Schumacher: DNF; Rubens Barrichello: 1st, FL

HUNGARIAN GP, HUNGARORING
Michael Schumacher: Pole, 2nd; Rubens Barrichello: 4th

BELGIAN GP, SPA-FRANCORCHAMPS
Michael Schumacher: 2nd; Rubens Barrichello: DNF, FL

ITALIAN GP, MONZA
Michael Schumacher: Pole, 1st; Rubens Barrichello: DNF

US GP, INDIANAPOLIS
Michael Schumacher: Pole, 1st; Rubens Barrichello: 2nd

JAPANESE GP, SUZUKA
Michael Schumacher: Pole, 1st; Rubens Barrichello: 4th

MALAYSIAN GP, SEPANG
Michael Schumacher: Pole, 1st; Rubens Barrichello: 3rd

4th in championship, 62 points (1st Michael Schumacher 108)

2001
Scuderia Ferrari, Formula One, Ferrari F2001

AUSTRALIAN GP, MELBOURNE
Michael Schumacher: Pole, 1st, FL; Rubens Barrichello: 3rd

MALAYSIAN GP, SEPANG
Michael Schumacher: Pole, 1st; Rubens Barrichello: 2nd

BRAZILIAN GP, INTERLAGOS
Michael Schumacher: Pole, 2nd; Rubens Barrichello: DNF

SAN MARINO GP, IMOLA
Michael Schumacher: DNF; Rubens Barrichello: 3rd

SPANISH GP, BARCELONA
Michael Schumacher: Pole, 1st, FL; Rubens Barrichello: DNF

AUSTRIAN GP, A1-RING
Michael Schumacher: Pole, 2nd; Rubens Barrichello: 3rd

MONACO GP, MONTE CARLO
Michael Schumacher: 1st; Rubens Barrichello: 2nd

CANADIAN GP, MONTREAL
Michael Schumacher: Pole, 2nd; Rubens Barrichello: DNF

EUROPEAN GP, NÜRBURGRING
Michael Schumacher: Pole, 1st; Rubens Barrichello: 5th

FRENCH GP, MAGNY-COURS
Michael Schumacher: 1st; Rubens Barrichello: 3rd

BRITISH GP, SILVERSTONE
Michael Schumacher: Pole, 2nd; Rubens Barrichello: 3rd

GERMAN GP, HOCKENHEIM
Michael Schumacher: DNF; Rubens Barrichello: 2nd

HUNGARIAN GP, HUNGARORING
Michael Schumacher: Pole, 1st; Rubens Barrichello: 2nd

BELGIAN GP, SPA-FRANCORCHAMPS
Michael Schumacher: 1st, FL; Rubens Barrichello: 5th

ITALIAN GP, MONZA
Michael Schumacher: 4th; Rubens Barrichello: 2nd

US GP, INDIANAPOLIS
Michael Schumacher: Pole, 2nd; Rubens Barrichello: 15th

JAPANESE GP, SUZUKA
Michael Schumacher: Pole, 1st; Rubens Barrichello: 5th

3rd in championship, 56 points (1st Michael Schumacher 123)

2002
Scuderia Ferrari, Formula One, Ferrari F2001/F2002

AUSTRALIAN GP, MELBOURNE
Michael Schumacher: 1st; Rubens Barrichello: Pole, DNF

MALAYSIAN GP, SEPANG
Michael Schumacher: 3rd; Rubens Barrichello: DNF

BRAZILIAN GP, INTERLAGOS
Michael Schumacher: 1st; Rubens Barrichello: DNF

SAN MARINO GP, IMOLA
Michael Schumacher: 1st; Rubens Barrichello: 2nd, FL

SPANISH GP, BARCELONA
Michael Schumacher: 1st; Rubens Barrichello: DNS

AUSTRIAN GP, A1-RING
Michael Schumacher: 1st; Rubens Barrichello: Pole, 2nd

MONACO GP, MONTE CARLO
Michael Schumacher: 2nd; Rubens Barrichello: 7th, FL

CANADIAN GP, MONTREAL
Michael Schumacher: 1st; Rubens Barrichello: 3rd

EUROPEAN GP, NÜRBURGRING
Michael Schumacher: 2nd; Rubens Barrichello: 1st

BRITISH GP, SILVERSTONE
Michael Schumacher: 1st; Rubens Barrichello: 2nd, FL

FRENCH GP, MAGNY-COURS
Michael Schumacher: 1st; Rubens Barrichello: DNS

GERMAN GP, HOCKENHEIM
Michael Schumacher: 1st; Rubens Barrichello: 4th

HUNGARIAN GP, HUNGARORING
Michael Schumacher: 2nd; Rubens Barrichello: Pole, 1st

BELGIAN GP, SPA-FRANCORCHAMPS
Michael Schumacher: 1st; Rubens Barrichello: 2nd

ITALIAN GP, MONZA
Michael Schumacher: 2nd; Rubens Barrichello: 1st, FL

US GP, INDIANAPOLIS
Michael Schumacher: 2nd; Rubens Barrichello: 1st, FL

JAPANESE GP, SUZUKA
Michael Schumacher: 1st; Rubens Barrichello: 2nd

2nd in championship, 77 points (1st Michael Schumacher 144)

2003
Scuderia Ferrari, Formula One, Ferrari F2002B/F2003-GA

AUSTRALIAN GP, MELBOURNE
Michael Schumacher: Pole, 4th; Rubens Barrichello: DNF

MALAYSIAN GP, SEPANG
Michael Schumacher: 6th, FL; Rubens Barrichello: 2nd

BRAZILIAN GP, INTERLAGOS
Michael Schumacher: DNF; Rubens Barrichello: Pole, DNF, FL

SAN MARINO GP, IMOLA
Michael Schumacher: Pole, 1st, FL; Rubens Barrichello: 3rd

SPANISH GP, BARCELONA
Michael Schumacher: Pole, 1st; Rubens Barrichello: 3rd, FL

AUSTRIAN GP, A1-RING
Michael Schumacher: Pole, 1st, FL; Rubens Barrichello: 3rd

MONACO GP, MONTE CARLO
Michael Schumacher: 3rd; Rubens Barrichello: 8th

CANADIAN GP, MONTREAL
Michael Schumacher: 1st; Rubens Barrichello: 5th

EUROPEAN GP, NÜRBURGRING
Michael Schumacher: 5th; Rubens Barrichello: 3rd

FRENCH GP, MAGNY-COURS
Michael Schumacher: 3rd; Rubens Barrichello: 7th

BRITISH GP, SILVERSTONE
Michael Schumacher: 4th; Rubens Barrichello: Pole, 1st, FL

GERMAN GP, HOCKENHEIM
Michael Schumacher: 7th; Rubens Barrichello: DNF

HUNGARIAN GP, HUNGARORING
Michael Schumacher: 8th; Rubens Barrichello: DNF

ITALIAN GP, MONZA
Michael Schumacher: Pole, 1st, FL; Rubens Barrichello: 3rd

US GP, INDIANAPOLIS
Michael Schumacher: 1st, FL; Rubens Barrichello: DNF

JAPANESE GP, SUZUKA
Michael Schumacher: 8th; Rubens Barrichello: Pole, 1st

4th in championship, 65 points (1st Michael Schumacher 93)

2004
Scuderia Ferrari, Formula One, Ferrari F2004

AUSTRALIAN GP, MELBOURNE
Michael Schumacher: Pole, 1st, FL; Rubens Barrichello: 2nd

MALAYSIAN GP, SEPANG
Michael Schumacher: Pole, 1st; Rubens Barrichello: 4th

BAHRAIN GP, SAKHIR
Michael Schumacher: Pole, 1st, FL; Rubens Barrichello: 2nd

SAN MARINO GP, IMOLA
Michael Schumacher: 1st, FL; Rubens Barrichello: 6th

SPANISH GP, BARCELONA
Michael Schumacher: Pole, 1st, FL; Rubens Barrichello: 2nd

MONACO GP, MONTE CARLO
Michael Schumacher: DNF, FL; Rubens Barrichello: 3rd

EUROPEAN GP, NÜRBURGRING
Michael Schumacher: Pole, 1st; Rubens Barrichello: 2nd

CANADIAN GP, MONTREAL
Michael Schumacher: 1st; Rubens Barrichello: 2nd, FL

US GP, INDIANAPOLIS
Michael Schumacher: 1st; Rubens Barrichello: Pole, 2nd, FL

FRENCH GP, MAGNY-COURS
Michael Schumacher: 1st, FL; Rubens Barrichello: 3rd

BRITISH GP, SILVERSTONE
Michael Schumacher: 1st, FL; Rubens Barrichello: 3rd

GERMAN GP, HOCKENHEIM
Michael Schumacher: Pole, 1st; Rubens Barrichello: DNF

HUNGARIAN GP, HUNGARORING
Michael Schumacher: Pole, 1st, FL; Rubens Barrichello: 2nd

BELGIAN GP, SPA-FRANCORCHAMPS
Michael Schumacher: 2nd; Rubens Barrichello: 3rd

ITALIAN GP, MONZA
Michael Schumacher: 2nd; Rubens Barrichello: Pole, 1st, FL

CHINESE GP, SHANGHAI
Michael Schumacher: 12th, FL; Rubens Barrichello: Pole, 1st

JAPANESE GP, SUZUKA
Michael Schumacher: Pole, 1st; Rubens Barrichello: DNF, FL

BRAZILIAN GP, INTERLAGOS
Michael Schumacher: 7th; Rubens Barrichello: Pole, 3rd

2nd in championship, 114 points (1st Michael Schumacher 148)

INDEX